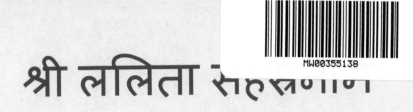

श्री ललिता सहस्रनाम

Sri Lalita Sahasranama

Munindra (Munnan) Misra

PARTRIDGE
A Penguin Random House Company

To order additional copies of this book, contact
Partridge India
000 800 10062 62
orders.india@partridgepublishing.com

www.partridgepublishing.com/india

Dedicated to my sister

Jyoti

ॐ

श्री गणेशाय

नमः

Contents

Lalita Sahasranama

Introduction

Lalita Sahasranama Stotra in *Brahmanda Puran* be,
Given to Rishi Agastya by Lord Hayagriva certainly,
Hayagriva an incarnation of Lord Vishnu does be,
He who the storehouse of complete knowledge be.
1

Agastya, sad with ignorant, pleasure seekers be,
Worshipped *Devi Kamakshi* - revered *Devi Shakti*,
Pleading for a solution to uplift masses clearly,
Hayagriva appeared, advised him, worship Devi.
2

Lalita Sahasranama stotra the best way does be,
To attain both spiritual, material upliftment truly,
Conveyed by sage Vyasya Maharishi certainly,
By vagdevatas under Laita's direction definitely.
3

Other Sahasranamas composed by Vyasa Maharishi,
Hayagriva has taught thousand Lalita names holy,
Lalita Sahasranama also *Rahasya Nama Sahasra* be,
Phala Stuti the effect of chanting it unquestionably.
4

http://en.wikipedia.org/wiki/File:Ardhanari.jpg

ॐ अस्य श्री ललिता दिव्य सहस्रनाम स्तोत्र महामंत्रस्य,
वशिन्यादि वाग्देवता ऋषयः, अनुष्टुप् छंदः,

श्री ललिता पराभट्टारिका महा त्रिपुर सुंदरी देवता,
ऐं बीजं, क्लीं शक्तिः, सौः कीलकं, मम धर्मार्थ

काम मोक्ष चतुर्विध फलपुरुषार्थ सिद्ध्यर्थं ललिता
त्रिपुरसुंदरी पराभट्टारिका सहस्र नाम जपे विनियोगः

Dhyanam

ध्यानं

अरुणां करुणा तरंगिताक्षीं धृतपाशांकुश पुष्पबाणचापाम् ।
अणिमादिभि रावृतां मयूखैः अहमित्येव विभावये भवानीम् ॥ १ ॥

Arunam Karuna thrangitakshim dhrutha –pasangusa-pushpabana-chapam,
Animadhibhi-ravrutham mayukai –raha mityeva vibhavaye Bhavanim.

1.

Goddess Bhavani has rising sun hue truly,
Her eyes which waves of real mercy do be,
Bow - sweet cane, arrows - soft flowers be,
Pasanugusa in hands, surrounded by devotees.

- 1 -

ध्यायेत् पद्मासनस्थां विकसितवदनां पद्म पत्रायताक्षीं

हेमाभां पीतवस्त्रां करकलित लसमद्धेमपद्मां वरांगीम् ।

सर्वालंकारयुक्तां सकलमभयदां भक्तनम्रां भवानीं

श्री विद्यां शांतमूर्ति सकल सुरसुतां सर्वसंपत्-प्रदात्रीम् ॥ २ ॥

Dyayeth padmasanastham vikasitha vadanam padma pathrayathakshim,
Hemabham peethavasthram karakalitha-lasadhema padmam varangim,
Sarvalangara yuktham saththam abhayadam bhaktha namram bhavanim.
Srividyam santhamuthim sakala suranutham sarva sampat pradhatrim.

2.

Divine Goddess seated on lotus with petal eyes be,
Golden hued, has lotus flowers in Her hand plainly,
Who bow before Her, dispels fear of the devotees,
Embodiment of peace, knowledge, wish granter be.

- 2 -

सकुंकुम विलेपना मलिकचुंबि कस्तूरिकां

समंद हसितेक्षणां सशरचाप पाशांकुशाम् ।

अशेष जनमोहिनी मरुणमाल्य भूषोज्ज्वलां

जपाकुसुम भासुरां जपविधौ स्मरे दंबिकाम् ॥ ३ ॥

Sakumkumalepana –malikachumbi-Kasthurikam,
Samanda hasithekshanam sashra chapa pasangusam,
Asesha jana mohinim –maruna malya bhoosham bara,
Japa-kusuma-basuram japa vidhou smarathembikam.

3.

I meditate on Mother, whose eyes smiling be,
Holding arrow, bow, noose and goad visibly,
She glitters with red garlands, ornaments surly,
With *kumkum* on her forehead, red as japa[1] be.
- 3 -

सिंधूरारुण विग्रहां त्रिणयनां माणिक्य मौलिस्फुर-

त्तारानायक शेखरां स्मितमुखी मापीन वक्षोरुहाम् ।

पाणिभ्या मलिपूर्णं रत्न चषकं रक्तोत्पलं बिभ्रतीं

सौम्यां रत्नघटस्थ रक्त चरणां ध्यायेत्परामंबिकाम् ॥ ४ ॥

Sindhuraruna vigraham trinayanam manikya mouli spurath
Thara Nayaga sekaram smitha mukhi mapina vakshoruham,
Panibhayam alipoorna ratna chashakam rakthothpalam vibhrathim,
Soumyam ratna gatastha raktha charanam, dhyayeth paramambikam.

4.

I meditate on Ambika - with saffron coloured body,
With three eyes, jeweled crown , moon adorned be,
Charming smile, firm breasts, with reddish flowers be,
Who is ocean of peace, her feet on jeweled stand be.
- 4 -

---

[1] flower

लमित्यादि पंच्हपूजां विभावयेत्

लं पृथिवी तत्त्वात्मिकायै श्री ललितादेव्यै

गंधं परिकल्पयामि

हम् आकाश तत्त्वात्मिकायै श्री ललितादेव्यै

पुष्पं परिकल्पयामि

यं वायु तत्त्वात्मिकायै श्री ललितादेव्यै

धूपं परिकल्पयामि

रं वह्नि तत्त्वात्मिकायै श्री ललितादेव्यै

दीपं परिकल्पयामि

वम् अमृत तत्त्वात्मिकायै श्री ललितादेव्यै

अमृत नैवेद्यं परिकल्पयामि

सं सर्व तत्त्वात्मिकायै श्री ललितादेव्यै

तांबूलादि सर्वोपचारान् परिकल्पयामि

http://en.wikipedia.org/wiki/Tripura_Sundari

गुरू ब्रह्मा, गुरू विष्णु, गुरू देवो महेश्वरः।
गुरुस्साक्षात परम ब्रह्मा तस्मै श्री गुरवे नामः॥

Guru the darkness dispeller, Guru Brahma the Creator be,
Guru Vishnu the Preserver; Guru Shiv the Transformer be,
Guru, the Supreme Being in human form – our savour be,
My salutations, awe, gratitude to that Divine Teacher be.

- 5 -

1st Shathaka

Shloka 1.

श्रीमाता श्रीमहाराज्ञी श्रीमद्सिंहासनेश्वरी
चिदग्निकुण्डसंभूता देवकार्य्यसमुद्यता ॥१

Shree Maathaa Shree maha-raajnee Shreemat-simhaasana-eswaree
Chit-agni-kundha-sambhoothaa Deva-kaarya-sam-udyathaa

1.

[2]To the mother of wealth all glories be,
From whom comes all wealth and glory,
[3]The great queen of the ultimate truth be,
[4]Seated on throne of the universe – Glory.
- 1 -

[5]Who arises from radiance real truth truly,
Who in devotee illuminates knowledge fully,
Frees him from darkness of ignorance truly,
With lamp of knowledge ends darkness* fully**.
- 2 -

[6]She who manifests to destroy evil – Glory,
Who strives to destroy evil in heart of devote,
Arjun, when virtue fades and evil grows truly,
Then I come as the conscience undoubtedly*
- 3 -

---

[2] श्रीमाता *Shree Maathaa*

[3] श्रीमहाराज्ञी *Shree-maha-raajnee*

[4] श्रीमद्सिंहासनेश्वरी *Shreemat-simhaasana-eswaree*

[5] चिदग्निकुण्डसंभूता *Chit-agni-kunda-sambhoothaa;* * *ignorance;* ** *Bhagavad Gita: Sloka Chapter*

[6] देवकार्य्यसमुद्यता *Deva-kaarya-sam-udyathaa;* * *Bhagavad Gita /*

Shloka 2.

उद्यत्भानुसहस्राभा चतुर्बाहुसमन्विता
रागस्वरूपपाशाढ्या क्रोधाकाराङ्कुशोज्ज्वला ॥२

Udyath-bhaanu-sahara-aabhaa Chatu-r-baahu-sama-anwithaa
Raga-swa-roopa-paasha-aadhya Kroedha-aakaara-angusha-o-ujjwalaa

2.

[7]Who enlightens and destroys evil of devotee,
[8]With four arms in all directions destroys evil fully,
[9]She the cause of love and attachment in life be,
[10]She carries stick of anger to destroy all surely.

- 4 -

Shloka 3.

मनोरूपेक्षुकोदण्डा पञ्चतन्मात्रसायका
निजारुणप्रभापूरमज्जद्ब्रह्माण्डमण्डला ॥३

Mana-o-roopa-e-ikshu-koethandaa Pancha-than-maatra-saayakaa
Nijaa-aruna-prabhaa-poora-majjath-brahmaanda-mandalaa

3.

[11]Who the mind of all living beings – Glory,
[12]Who controls five senses* clearly – Glory,
Who helps life appreciate them by mind truly,
[13]In Her light pink glow universe immersed be.

- 5 -

---

[7] उद्यत्भानुसहस्राभा Udyath-bhaanu-sahara-aabhaa

[8] चतुर्बाहुसमन्विता Chatu-r-baahu-sama-anwithaa

[9] रागस्वरूपपाशाढ्या Raga-swa-roopa-paasha-aadhya

[10] क्रोधाकाराङ्कुशोज्ज्वला Kroedha-aakaara-angusha-o-ujjwalaa

[11] मनोरूपेक्षुकोदण्डा Mana-o-roopa-e-ikshu-koethandaa; ikshu = stem of the sugar cane

[12] पञ्चतन्मात्रसायका Pancha-than-maatra-saayakaa; Pancha = five senses sight, taste, smell, touch and sound

[13] निजारुणप्रभापूरमज्जद्ब्रह्माण्डमण्डला Nijaa-aruna-prabhaa-poora-majjath-brahmaanda-mandalaa

Shloka 4.

चंपकाशोकपुन्नागसौगन्धिकलसत्कचा
कुरुविन्दमणिश्रेणीकनत्कोटीरमण्डिता ॥४

Champakaa-ashoka-punnaga-soungandika-lasath-kachaa
Kuruvinda-mani-sraenee-kanath-koeteera-mandithaa

4.

[14]Her hair the fragrance of flowers heavenly,
She the originator from whom all fragrances be,
[15]She the real crown who is ornamented wholly,
She source of all wealth, gems, prized stones be.

- 6 -

Shloka 5.

अष्टमीचन्द्रविभ्राजदलिकस्थलशोभिता
मुखचन्द्रकलङ्काभ मृगनाभिविशेषका ॥५

Ashtamee-chandra-vibhraajath-alika-st'thala-shoebhithaa
Mukha-chandra-kalanga-aabha-mr'ga-naabhee-visheshakaa

5.

[16]She adorned with half moon illuminence be,
[17]Her face moon's beauty tainted by a tilak* be,
She who has manifested as everything – Glory,
That which is beautiful in this universe surely.

- 7 -

---

[14] चंपकाशोकपुन्नागसौगन्धिकलसत्कचा Champakaa-ashoka-punnaaga-soungandika-lasath-kachaa
[15] कुरुविन्दमणिश्रेणीकनत्कोटीरमण्डिता Kuruvinda-mani-sraenee-kanath-koeteera-mandithaa
[16] अष्टमीचन्द्रविभ्राजदलिकस्थलशोभिता Ashtamee-chandra-vibhraajath-alika-st'thala-shoebhithaa
[17] मुखचन्द्रकलङ्काभ मृगनाभिविशेषका Mukha-chandra-kalanga-aabha-mr'ga-naabhee-visheshakaa;
* kasturi

श्री ललिता सहस्रनाम

Shloka 6.

वदनस्मरमांगल्यगृहतोरणचिल्लिका
वक्त्रलक्ष्मीपरीवाह चलन्मीनाभलोचना ॥६

Vadana-smara-maangalya-gr'ha-thoerana-chillikaa
Vakthra-lakshmee-pareevaaha-chalan-meena-aabha-loechanaa

6.

[18]She with extremely beautiful eye brows be,
Its movement changes universal cause truly,
As man swayed by *kama deva* spell bound be,
[19]She with extremely beautiful eyes does be.
- 8 -

Shloka 7.

नवचंपकपुष्पाभा नासादण्डविराजिता
ताराकान्तितिरस्कारिनासाभरणभासुरा ॥७

Nava-champaka-pushpa-aabha-naasa-danda-viraajithaa
Thaara-kaanthi thiraskaari-naasa-aabharana-bhaasuraa

7.

[20]Her nose fresh *champak* flower does be,
Sublime and beautiful – to Her all Glory,
[21]She who with the beautiful nose stud be,
To Her heavenly grace – all the Glory.
- 9 -

---

[18] *वदनस्मरमांगल्यगृहतोरणचिल्लिका* Vadana-smara-maangalya-gr'ha-thoerana-chillikaa;
Smara = kaama-deva

[19] *वक्त्रलक्ष्मीपरीवाह चलन्मीनाभलोचना* Vakthra-lakshmee-pareevaaha-chalan-meena-
aabha-loechanaa; मीनः = fish

[20] *नवचंपकपुष्पाभा नासादण्डविराजिता* Nava-champaka-pushpa-aabha-naasa-danda-
viraajithaa

[21] *ताराकान्तितिरस्कारिनासाभरणभासुरा* Thaara-kaanthi thiraskaari-naasa-aabharana-
bhaasuraa

Shloka 8.

कदंबमञ्जरीक्ॢप्तकर्ण्णपूरमनोहरा

ताटङ्कयुगलीभूततपनोडुपमण्डला ॥८

Kadamba-manjari-kniptha-karna-poora-mana-o-hara
Thaatanka-yugalee-bhootha-tapan-o-udupa-mandalaa

8.

[22]She who beautiful with a bunch of flowers be,
Of the *kadamba* trees with her ear studs surely,
[23]Whose ear studs the sun and the moon do be,
Who manifests as universe – to Her all Glory.

- 10 -

Shloka 9.

पद्मरागशिलादर्शपरिभाविकपोलभूः

नवविद्रुमबिंबश्रीन्यक्कारिरदनच्छदा ॥९

Padma-raaga-shila-aadarsha-paribhavi-kapola- bhooh
Nava-vidruma-bimba-sree-nyakkaary-radana-ch'chadaa

9.

[24]She who with the most beautiful cheeks be,
Smoother than gem, as polished mirror glittery,
[25]Whose lips outshine the redness certainly,
That of fresh coral and bimba fruit confidently.

- 11 -

---

[22] कदंबमञ्जरीक्ॢप्तकर्ण्णपूरमनोहरा Kadamba-manjari-kniptha-karna-poora-mana-o-hara

[23] ताटङ्कयुगलीभूततपनोडुपमण्डला Thaatanka-yugalee-bhootha-tapan-o-udupa-mandalaa

[24] पद्मरागशिलादर्शपरिभाविकपोलभू Padma-raaga-shila-aadarsha-paribhavi-kapola- bhoo

[25] नवविद्रुमबिम्बश्रीन्यक्कारिरदनच्छदा Nava-vidruma-bimba-sree-nyakkaary-radana-ch'chadaa

Shloka 10.

शुद्धविद्याङ्कुराकारद्विजपङ्क्तिद्वयोज्वला
कर्प्पूरवीटिकामोदसमाकर्षिदिगन्तरा ॥१०

Shudha-vidya-ankura-aakaara-dwija-pankthi-dwaya-o-ujjwala
Karpoora-veetikaa-aamoeda-sama-aakarshitha-dig-antharaa

10.

[26]She who with extremely beautiful teeth be,
[27]Who chews beetles leaves fragrant surely,
The fragrance attracts in all directions truly,
She who attracts everyone to herself clearly.
- 12 -

Shloka 11.

निजसल्लापमाधुर्य्यविनिर्भसितकच्छपी
मन्दस्मितप्रभापूरमज्जत्कामेशमानसा ॥११

Nija-sallaapa-maadhurya-vini-r-bharsitha -kach'chapee
Manda-smitha-prabhaa-poora-majjath-kaama-esa-maanasa

11.

[28]She whose voice with sweetness be,
That it belittles her veena's sound surely,
Her voice soothens heart of her devotee,
[29]She who with the beautiful smile does be.
- 13 -

Who supreme over all passions does be,
Who bring all passions under control fully,
Who overcoming desires and anger truly,
Who Self-aware – She glad for that devotee.
- 14 -

---

[26] शुद्धविद्याङ्कुराकारद्विजपङ्क्तिद्वयोज्वला Shudha-vidya-ankura-aakaara-dwija-pankthi-dwaya-o-ujjwala
[27] कर्प्पूरवीटिकामोदसमाकर्षिदिगन्तरा Karpoora-veetikaa-aamoeda-sama-aakarshitha-dig-antharaa
[28] निजसल्लापमाधुर्य्यविनिर्भसितकच्छपी Nija-sallaapa-maadhurya-vini-r-bharsitha -kach'chapee
[29] मन्दस्मितप्रभापूरमज्जत्कामेशमानसा Manda-smitha-prabhaa-poora-majjath-kaama-esa-maanasa

Shloka 12.

अनाकलितसादृश्यचिबुकश्रीविराजिता
कामेशबद्धमांगल्यसूत्रशोभितकन्धरा ॥१२

*Anaakalitha-saadr'shya-chubuka-sree-viraajithaa
kaama-esa-badha-maangalya-soothra-shoebhitha-kandharaa*

12.

[30]Her beautiful chin has no comparision truly,
[31]She who with the very beautiful neck does be,
She has all passions, desires sublimed fully,
She who supreme over all his passions be.
- 15 -

She who can be reached straightforwardly,
Known, influenced by them who surrender fully,
All desires, passions in perfect sublimation be,
To Her I bow who has all grace – sautation be.
- 16 -

Shloka 13.

कनकाङ्गदकेयूरकमनीयभुजान्विता
रत्नग्रैवेयचिन्ताकलोलमुक्ताफलान्विता ॥१३

*Kanaka-angada-kaeyoora-kamaneeya-bhuja-anwithaa
Rathna-graivaeya-chinthaka-loela-muktha-ppala-anwithaa*

13.

[32]Who with beautiful arms ornaments decked be,
She who gives to the devotee of all wealth freely,
Also knowledge wealth which she can give only,
[33]She decked with gems, pearls, prized stone clearly.
- 17 -

---

[30] अनाकलितसादृश्यचिबुकश्रीविराजिता Anaakalitha-saadr'shya-chubuka-sree-viraajithaa

[31] कामेशबद्धमांगल्यसूत्रशोभितकन्धरा Kaama-esa-badha-maangalya-soothra-shoebhitha-kandharaa

[32] कनकाङ्गदकेयूरकमनीयभुजान्विता Kanaka-angada-kaeyoora-kamaneeya-bhuja-anwithaa

[33] रत्नग्रैवेयचिन्ताकलोलमुक्ताफलान्विता Ratna-graivaeya-chinthaaka-loela-muktha-ppala-anwithaa

She to whom belongs all wealth unquestionably,
Including the precious stones and gems surely,
And also total wealth of knowledge completely,
Which alone leads to utmost truth – the devotee.
- 18 -

Shloka 14.

कामेश्वरप्रेमरत्नमणिप्रतिपणस्तनी

नाभ्यालवालरोमालिलताफलकुचद्वयी ॥१४

Kaama-eswara-prema-ratna-mani-prathi-pana-sthanee
Naabhy-aalavaala-roema-ali-latha-ppala-kucha-dwayee

14.

[34]She controls passions, desires – its lord be,
She who gives sublime passions to devotee,
In whom devotee in full surrender, rests fully,
[35]She with a beautiful navel and bosom does be.
- 19 -

Shloka 15.

लक्ष्यरोमलताधारतासमुन्नेयमद्ध्यमा

स्तनभारदलन्मद्ध्यपट्टबन्धवलित्रया ॥१५

Lakshya-roema-lathaa-aadharathaa samunnaeya- madhyamaa
Sthana-bhaara-dalan-madhya-patta-bandha-vali-thrayaa

15.

[36]She who has very beautiful mid body,
Her waist as creeper like hairs therein be,
[37]Her three stripes created to protect belly,
Her tiny waist from her breasts so heavy.
- 20 -

---

[34] *कामेश्वरप्रेमरत्नमणिप्रतिपणस्तनी* Kaama-eswara-prema-ratna-mani-prathi-pana-sthanee

[35] *नाभ्यालवालरोमालिलताफलकुचद्वयी* Naabhy-aalavaala-roema-ali-latha-ppala-kucha-dwayee

[36] *लक्ष्यरोमलताधारतासमुन्नेयमद्ध्यमा* Lakshya-roema-lathaa-aadharathaa sam-unnaeya-madhyamaa

[37] *स्तनभारदलन्मद्ध्यपट्टबन्धवलित्रया* Sthana-bhaara-dalan-madhya-patta-bandha-vali-thrayaa

Shloka 16.

अरुणारुणकौसुंभवस्त्रभास्वत्कटीतटी

रत्नकिङ्किणिकारम्यरशनाधामभूषिता ॥१६

Aruna-aruna-kousumbha-vasthra-bhaaswath-katee-thatee
Ratna-kinginikaa-ramya-rashana-daama-bhooshithaa

16.

[38]She has a red shining dress on waist clearly,
She who worshipped with a red dress only,
[39]Her waist with thread of beautiful gems be,
She who with much decorations certainly.

- 21 -

Shloka 17.

कामेशज्ञातसौभाग्यमार्द्वोरुद्वयान्विता

माणिक्यमकुटाकारजानुद्वयविराजिता ॥१७

Kaama-esa-jnaatha-soubhaagya-maard'dava-ooru-dwaya-anwithaa
Maanikya-makuta-aakaara-jaanu-dwaya-viraajithaa

17.

[40]She whose passions under control be,
Who lord of all His desires, passions be,
Whose unseen beauty appreciated only,
By those whose passions sublimed do be,

- 22 -

Her pretty thighs known to her consort only,
[41]She who with knees which very beautiful be,
As the Manikya crown below her thighs be,
They as lids fully decorated with fine rubies.

- 23 -

---

[38] अरुणारुणकौसुंभवस्त्रभास्वत्कटीतटी Aruna-aruna-kousumbha-vasthra-bhaaswath-katee-thatee

[39] रत्नकिङ्किणिकारम्यरशनाधामभूषिता Ratna-kinginikaa-ramya-rashana-daama-bhooshithaa

[40] कामेशज्ञातसौभाग्यमार्द्वोरुद्वयान्विता Kaama-esa-jnaatha-soubhaagya-maard'dava-ooru-dwaya-anwithaa

[41] माणिक्यमकुटाकारजानुद्वयविराजिता Maanikya-makuta-aakaara-jaanu-dwaya-viraajithaa

---

Shloka 18.

इन्द्रगोपपरिक्षिप्तस्मरतूणाभजंघिका

गूडगुल्फा कूर्म्मपृष्टजयिष्णुप्रपदान्विता ॥१८

Indragoepa-parikshiptha-smara-thoona-aabha-janghikaa
Gooda-gulppaa Koorma-pr'sht'ta jaysishnu-pra-pada-anwithaa

18.

[42]She with extremely beautiful calves does be,
[43]She who whose ankles are hidden entirely,
She hides self from human beings ordinary,
[44]Her feet extremely smooth at the top do be.
- 24 -

Smoother than the shell of a tortoise clearly,
She whose feet be hugged by the devotee ,
And without dread or fear of getting hurt be,
Who protects devotee who seeks her surely.
- 25 -

Shloka 19.

नखदीधितिसंच्छन्ननमज्जनतमोगुणा

पदद्वयप्रभाजालपराकृतसरोरुहा ॥१९

Nakha-deedhithi-samch'channa-nama-jana-thama-o-gunaa
Pada-dwaya-prabhaa-jaala-paraakr'tha-sara-ooruhaa

19.

[45]Her nails' illumination sufficient do be,
To destroy the darkness of Her devotees,
She who grants light of knowledge truly,
To those who pursue her with sincerity.
- 26 -

---

[42] इन्द्रगोपपरिक्षिप्तस्मरतूणाभजंघिका Indragoepa-parikshiptha-smara-thoona-aabha-janghikaa

[43] गूडगुल्फा Gooda-gulppaa

[44] कूर्म्मपृष्टजयिष्णुप्रपदान्विता Koorma-pr'sht'ta jayishnu-pra-pada-anwithaa

[45] नखदीधितिसंच्छन्ननमज्जनतमोगुणा Nakha-deedhithi-samch'channa-nama-jana-thama-o-gunaa

[46]She who with extremely beautiful feet be,
Which defeats the lotus flower's beauty,
On whom entire universe supported be,
She at whose feet falls all the devotee.
- 27 -

Shloka 20.

शिञ्जानमणिमञ्जीरमण्डितश्रीपदांबुजा
मरालीमन्दगमना महालावण्यशेवधि: ॥२०

Shinjaana-mani-manjeera-manditha-sree-pada-ambujaa
Maraalee-manda-gamana Maha-laavanya-shaevathee

20.

[47]She with anklets jingle while walking be,
Devotee like music of anklet jingling truly,
[48]She who with a beautiful gait does be,
[49] She the source of all beauty does be.
- 28 -

---

[46] पदद्वयप्रभाजालपराकृतसरोरुहा Pada-dwaya-prabhaa-jaala-paraakr'tha-sara-ooruhaa
[47] शिञ्जानमणिमञ्जीरमण्डितश्रीपदांबुजा Shinjaana-mani-manjeera-manditha-sree-pada-ambujaa
[48] मरालीमन्दगमना Maraalee-manda-gamana
[49] महालावण्यशेवधि: Maha-laavanya-shaevathee

Shloka 21.

सर्व्वारुणाऽनवद्याङ्गी सर्व्वाभरणभूषिता

शिवकामेश्वराङ्गस्था शिवा स्वाधीनवल्लभा ॥२१॥

Sarva-aruna-anawadya-angeee Sarva-aabharana-bhooshithaa
Shiva-kaama-eshwara-anga-st'tha Shivaa Swadheena -valabhaa

21.

[50]She who appreciated with pink by devotee,
[51]With everything worshippable about her be,
[52]She who adorned with many ornaments be,
Manifested in universe as rivers, oceans truly,
- 29 -

She the stars, sun, moon, whole universe be,
[53]She ruler controlling passions, desires be,
[54]She who with all does be and to her glory,
[55]She dear to devotee who free from wants be.
- 30 -

---

[50] सर्वारुणा *Sarva-aruna*

[51] अनवद्याङ्गी *Anawadya-angeee*

[52] सर्वाभरणभूषिता *Sarva-aabharana-bhooshithaa*

[53] शिवकामेश्वराङ्गस्था *Shiva-kaama-eshwara-anga-st'tha*

[54] शिवा *Shivaa*

[55] स्वाधीनवल्लभा *Swaadheena -valabhaa*

Shloka 22.

सुमेरुमद्ध्यशृंगस्था श्रीमन्नगरनायिका
चिन्तामणिगृहान्तस्था पञ्चब्रह्मासनस्थिता ॥२२॥

Sumaeru-madhya-shr'ngast'tha Sree-mat-nagara-naayikaa
Chintaa-mani-g'rha-antha-st'thaa Pancha-brahma-aasana-st'thithaa

22.

[56]She in the middle amid *ida* and *pingala* be,
[57]Queen of the kingdom, grants desires truly,
[58]She who grant every desire of the devotees,
[59]She seat on which universe bases itself surely.
- 31 -

Shloka 23.

महापद्माटवीसंस्था कदंबवनवासिनी
सुधासागरमद्ध्यस्था कामाक्षी कामदायिनी ॥२३॥

Maha-padma-adavee-samst'thaa Kadamba-vana-vaasinee
Sudhaa-saagara-madhya-st'thaa Kama-aakshee Kaama-daayinee

23.

[60]She manifests to devotee in meditation truly,
[61]She lives in a forest thick with Kadamba tree,
She not easily accessible to human's ordinary,
[62]She resides in midst of an ocean of nectar truly.
- 32 -

---

[56] सुमेरुमद्ध्यशृंगस्था Sumaeru-madhya-shr'ngast'tha

[57] श्रीमन्नगरनायिका Sree-mannagara-naayikaa

[58] चिन्तामणिगृहान्तस्था Chintaa-mani-g'rha-antha-st'tha

[59] पञ्चब्रह्मासनस्थिता Pancha-brahma-aasana-st'thithaa

[60] महापद्माटवीसंस्था Maha-padma-adavee-samst'thaa

[61] कदंबवनवासिनी Kadamba-vana-vaasine

[62] सुधासागरमद्ध्यस्था Sudhaa-saagara-madhya-st'thaa

श्री ललिता सहस्रनाम

She accessible to who very pure at heart do be,
The not pure and senseless do not see clearly,
[63]She grants desires, makes all possible surely,
[64]She who grants all desires by her grace only.

- 33 -

Shloka 24.

देवर्षिगणसंघातस्तूयमानात्मवैभवा

भण्डासुरवधोद्युक्तशक्तिसेनासमन्विता ॥२४

Devarshi-gana-sanghaatha-sthooya-maana-aathma-vaibhavaa
Bhanda-asura-vadha-udyukta-shakti-saena-sam-anwithaa

24.

[65]She revered by knowledgeable with divinity,
She source of all, through Her everything be,
[66]She has strength to destroy evil heart fully,
And enlighten devotee with knowledge truly.

- 34 -

---

[63] कामाक्षी Kama-aakshee

[64] कामदायिनी Kaama-daayinee

[65] देवर्षिगणसंघातस्तूयमानात्मवैभवा Devarshi-gana-sanghaatha-sthooya-maana-aathma-vaibhavaa

[66] भण्डासुरवधोद्युक्तशक्तिसेनासमन्विता Bhandha-asura-vadha-o-udyukta-shakti-saena-sama-anwithaa

---

Shloka 25.

संबल्करीसमारूढसिन्धुरव्रजसेवीता
अश्वारूढाधिष्ठिताश्वकोटिकोटिभिरावृता ॥२५

Sambalkaree-sam-aaroodha-sindhura-vraja-saevithaa
Ashwa-aaroodha-adhisht'titha-ashwa-koeti-koetibhi-r-aavr'thaa

25.

[67]She has an elephant army, gives wealth surely,
[68]She who served by a big army of horses be,
She with force and strength destroy evil wholly,
In the heart of devotee and illuminating it fully.
- 35 -

Shloka 26.

चक्रराजरथारूढसर्वायुधपरिष्कृता
गेयचक्ररथारूढमन्त्रिणीपरिसेविता ॥२६

Chakra-raaja-rat'tha-aaroodha-sarva-aayudha-parishkr'thaa
Gaeya-chakra-rat'tha-aaroodha-manthrinee-pari-saevithaa

26.

[69]She seated in chariot with weapons amply,
[70]She who served by those who are worthy,
By virtue of self-knowledge and heart purity,
She source of all, wise worship unreservedly.
- 36 -

---

[67] संबल्करीसमारूढसिन्धुरव्रजसेवीता Sambalkaree-sam-aaroodha-sindhura-vraja-saevithaa

[68] अश्वारूढाधिष्ठिताश्वकोटिकोटिभिरावृता Ashwa-aaroodha-adhisht'titha-ashwa-koeti-koetibhi-r-aavr'thaa

[69] चक्रराजरथारूढसर्वायुधपरिष्कृता Chakra-raaja-rat'tha-aaroodha-sarva-aayudha-parishkr'thaa

[70] गेयचक्ररथारूढमन्त्रिणीपरिसेविता Gaeya-chakra-rat'tha-aaroodha-manthrinee-pari-saevitha

---

Shloka 27.

किरिचक्ररथारूढदण्डनाथापुरस्कृता
ज्वालामालिनिकाक्षिप्तवह्निप्राकारमद्ध्यगा ॥२७

Kiri-chakra-rat'tha-aaroodha-danda-naat'thaa-apuraskr'thaa
Jwaala-maalini-kaakshiptha-vahni-praakaara-madhygaa

27.

[71]She protects from fears of life and death truly,
Her devotee free of life and death fear promptly
[72]She who is seated fortified by fire completely,
She gives proper insight to reach Her finally.

- 37 -

Shloka 28.

भण्डसैन्यवधोद्युक्तशक्तिविक्रमहर्षिता
नित्यापराक्रमाटोपनिरीक्षणसमुल्सुका ॥२८

Bhanda-syinya-vadha-udyukta-Shakti-vikrama-harshithaa
Nithyaa Parakrama-aatoepa-nireekshana-sam-ulsukaa

28.

[73]She in ecstacy ready to destroy evil forcefully,
For Her devotee who surrender in Her totally,
[74]Who try to acheive self, She watches intently,
Who control desires, passions - surrender fully.

- 38 -

---

[71] किरिचक्ररथारूढदण्डनाथापुरस्कृता *Kiri-chakra-rat'tha-aaroodha-danda-naat'thaa-apuraskr'thaa*
[72] ज्वालामालिनिकाक्षिप्तवह्निप्राकारमद्ध्यगा *Jwaala-maalini-kaakshiptha-vahni-praakaara-madhygaa*
[73] भण्डसैन्यवधोद्युक्तशक्तिविक्रमहर्षिता *Bhandha-sainya-vadha-udyukta-shakthi-vikrama-harshithaa*
[74] नित्यापराक्रमाटोपनिरीक्षणसमुल्सुका *Nithyaa Paraakrama-aatoepa-nireekshana-sam-ulsukaa*

Shloka 29.

भण्डपुत्रवधोद्युक्तबालाविक्रमनन्दिता
मन्त्रिण्यंबाविरचितविषम्गवधतोषिता ॥२९

Bhanda-puthra-vadha-udyukta-baala vikrama-nandithaa
Manthrini-ambaa- virachitha-visha-anga-vadha-thoeshithaa

29.

[75]She happy with who destroy all evil clearly,
Who intent on ending evil of passions fully,
[76]Who fight what destructive to goodness be,
Who strives for freedom from sense ecstasy.
- 39 -

Shloka 30.

विशुक्रप्राणहरणवाराहीवीर्य्यनन्दिता
कामेश्वरमुखालोककल्पित श्रीगणेश्वरा ॥३०

Vishukra-praana-harana-vaaraahee-veerya-nandithaa
Kaama-eswara-mukha-aaloeka-kalpitha-sree-gana-eswaraa

30.

[77]She happy with who free of attachement be,
Who considers Her the last refuge sincerely,
She the truth from which all created do be,
[78]She sees devotee who from wants is free.
- 40 -

---

[75] भण्डपुत्रवधोद्युक्तबालाविक्रमनन्दिता *Bhandha-puthra-vadha-udyukta-baala vikrama-nandithaa*

[76] मन्त्रिण्यम्बाविरचितविषम्गवधतोषिता *Manthrini-amba- virachitha-visha-anga-vadha-thoeshithaa*

[77] विशुक्रप्राणहरणवाराहीवीर्य्यनन्दिता *Vishukra-praana-harana-vaaraahee-veerya-nandithaa*

[78] कामेश्वरमुखालोककल्पित श्रीगणेश्वरा *Kaama-eswara-mukha-aaloeka-kalpitha-sree-gana-eswaraa*

Shloka 31.

महागणेशनिर्भिन्नविघ्नयन्त्रप्रहर्षिता

भण्डासुरेन्द्रनिर्म्मुक्तशस्त्रप्रत्यस्त्रवर्षिणी ॥३१

Maha-gana-esa-ni-r-bhinna-vigh'nna-yanthra-praharshithaa
Bhanda-asura-e-indra-ni-r-mukta-shastra-prathya-asthra-varshinee

31.

[79]She is happy with who contols wants fully,
She destroys all evil with her own power truly,
[80]She ends night ignorance of darkness clearly,
With illumination of knowledge of day surely.
- 41 -

Shloka 32.

कराङ्गुलिनखोल्पन्ननारायणदशाकृतिः

महापाशुपतास्त्राग्निनिर्द्ग्धासुरसैनिका ॥३२

Kara-anguli-nakha-ulpanna-narayana-dasa-akr'thih
Maha-paasu-patha-asthra-agni-ni-r-daghda-aasura-sainikaa

32.

[81]From Her the five states of life surely be,
And from Her states of creation came to be,
She the destroyer of evil forces with fire be,
[82]She removes darkness, enlightens devotee.
- 42 -

---

[79] *महागणेशनिर्भिन्नविघ्नयन्त्रप्रहर्षिता*Maha-gana-esa-ni-r-bhinna-vigh'nna-yanthra-
praharshithaa
[80] *भण्डासुरेन्द्रनिर्म्मुक्तशस्त्रप्रत्यस्त्रवर्षिणी*Bhanda-asura-e-indra-ni-r-mukta-shastra-prathya-
asthra-varshinee
[81] *कराङ्गुलिनखोल्पन्ननारायणदशाकृति* Kara-anguli-nakha-ulpanna-narayana-dasa-akr'thih;
*The five states of life: awareness, dream, sleep, what is beyond these three, the
ultimate state of becoming one with the supreme bliss; The states of creation:
creation, maintenance, dissolution, nothingness and then re-creation*
[82] *महापाशुपतास्त्राग्निनिर्द्ग्धासुरसैनिका*Maha-paasu-patha-asthra-agni-ni-r-daghda-aasura-
sainikaa

Shloka 33.

कामेश्वरास्त्रनिर्द्गग्धसभण्डासुरशून्यका
ब्रह्मोपेन्द्रमहेन्द्रादिदेवसंस्तुतवैभवा ॥३३

Kaama-ewara-asthra-ni-r-daghda-sa-bhanda-asura-shoonyakaa
Brahma-upaendra-maha-e-indra-aadi-deva-samsthutha-vaibhavaa

33.

She the lord of all His passions, desires only,
[83]Her devotees free from passions, desires be,
[84]She worshipped by Brahma, Indra, others deities,
Revered by worthy - free in mind, submitted fully.
- 43 -

Shloka 34.

हरनेत्राग्निसंदग्धकामसंजीवनौषधि:
श्रीमद्वाग्भवकूटैकस्वरूपमुखपङ्कजा ॥३४

Hara-naethra-agni-sam-dagdha-kaama-sanjeevan-oushadee
Sreemat-vaag-bhava-kooota-eka-swa-roopa-mukha-pankajaa

34.

[85]She the knowledge cure who burnt by wants be,
By problems of life born from desires, passions truly,
[86]She whose face has the form but unquestionably,
Of the first alphabets of the Sri Vidya Mantra surely.
- 44 -

---

[83] कामेश्वरास्त्रनिर्द्गग्धसभण्डासुरशून्यका Kaama-ewara-asthra-ni-r-dagha-sa-bhandha-asura-shoonyakaa

[84] ब्रह्मोपेन्द्रमहेन्द्रादिदेवसंस्तुतवैभवा Brahma-upaendra-maha-e-indra-aadi-deva-samsthutha-vaibhavaa

[85] हरनेत्राग्निसंदग्धकामसंजीवनौषधि Hara-naethra-agni-sam-dagdha-kaama-sanjeevan-oushadee

[86] श्रीमद्वाग्भवकूटैकस्वरूपमुखपङ्कजा Sreemat-vaag-bhava-koooda-eka-swa-roopa-mukha-pankajaa

---

श्री ललिता सहस्रनाम

Shloka 35.

कण्ठाध: कटिपर्य्यन्तमद्ध्यकूटस्वरूपिणी
शक्तिकूटैकतापन्नकट्यधोभागधारिणी ॥३५

Kant'ta-adhah Kati-pary-antha-madhya-koota-swa-roopinee
Shakti-koota-ekatha-aapanna-kati-adha-o-bhaaga-dhaarinee

35.

[87]She whose trunk from neck to hips has clearly,
Form of second alphabets of Sri Vidya Mantra truly,
[88]Her lower body last alphabets of Sri Vidya Mantra be,
Her body below the hips is the Shakti koota – Glory.
- 45 -

Shloka 36.

मूलमन्त्रात्मिका मूलकूटत्रयकलेभरा
कुलामृतैकरसिका कुलसङ्केतपालिनी ॥३६

Moola-manthra-aathmikaa Moola-koota-thraya-kalaebara
Kula-amr'tha-eka-rasikaa Kula-sangaetha-paalinee

36.

[89]She has form of the Shri Vidya mantra truly,
She the *Moola manthra* She is the cause – Glory,
[90]Her form three parts of Shri Vidya mantra be,
[91]She enjoys nectar when yogi in bliss does be.
- 46 -

---

[87] कण्ठाध: कटिपर्य्यन्तमद्ध्यकूटस्वरूपिणी Kant'ta-adhah Kati-pary-antha-madhya-koota-swa-roopinee

[88] शक्तिकूटैकतापन्नकट्यधोभागधारिणी Shakthi-koota-ekatha-aapanna-kati-adha-o-bhaaga-dhaarinee

[89] मूलमन्त्रात्मिका Moola-manthra-aathmikaa

[90] मूलकूटत्रयकलेभरा Moola-koota-thraya-kalaebara

[91] कुलामृतैकरसिका Kula-amr'tha-eka-rasikaa

She sees principles illuminated by *shastras* fully,
[92]She likes who deal with shastras' secret truly,
From them who have learned them correctly,
She herself the ultimate guide and teacher be.
- 47 -

Shloka 37.

कुलांगना कुलान्तस्था कौलिनी कुलयोगिनी
अकुला समयान्तस्था समयाचारतत्परा ॥३७

Kula-anganaa Kula-antha-st'thaa Koulinee Kula-yoeginee
Akulaa samaya-antha-st'thaa Samaya-aachara-thalparaa

37.

[93]She who does not appear before everyone easily,
She who is not known to the human mind ordinary,
[94]She subject of scriptures and known by them only,
[95]She worshipped in all homes, places, countries.
- 48 -

[96]She who present in all homes, places, clans be,
[97]She without particular clan, family, home, place be,
[98]She who exists in surrender and sublimation clearly,
[99]She fond of discipline lives in the heart of devotee.
- 49 -

---

[92] कुलसङ्केतपालिनी Kula-sangaetha-paalinee

[93] कुलांगना Kula-anganaa

[94] कुलान्तस्था Kula-antha-st'thaa

[95] कौलिनी Koulinee

[96] कुलयोगिनी Kula-yoeginee

[97] अकुला Akulaa

[98] समयान्तस्था Samaya-antha-st'thaa

[99] समयाचारतत्परा Samaya-aachara-thalparaa

Shloka 38.

मूलाधारैकनिलया ब्रह्मग्रन्थि विभेदिनी
मणिपूरान्तरुदिता विष्णुग्रन्थि विभेदिनी ॥३८

Moola-aadhaara-eka-nilayaa Brahma-granttthi-vibhaediniee
Mani-poora-antha-r-udithaa Vishnu-grantthi-vibhaethinee

38.

[100]She unawakened kundalinee at spine tip be,
Makes life possible to perform all actions fully,
[101]She helps us cross ties due to our birth clearly,
Remove obstacles that block spiritual gains truly.
- 50 -

[102]She is completely dressed in her elegant fineries
She manifests as he ascends levels certainly,
[103]She helps him to get beyond this level finally,
She helps cross ties due to position – all Glory.
- 51 -

---

[100] *मूलाधारैकनिलया Moola-aadhaara-eka-nilayaa*

[101] *ब्रह्मग्रन्थिविभेदिनी Brahma-grantthi-vibhaediniee*

[102] *मणिपूरान्तरुदिता Mani-poora-antha-r-udithaa*

[103] *विष्णुग्रन्थि विभेदिनी Vishnu-grantthi-vibhaethinee*

2nd Shathaka

Shloka 39.

आज्ञाचक्रान्तरालस्था रुद्रग्रन्थिविभेदिनी
सहस्रारांबुजारूढ़ा सुधासाराभिवर्षिणी ॥३९

Aajnaa-chakra-antharaala-st'thaa Rudra-grantthi-vibhaethinee
Sahasrara-amuja-aaroodhaa Sudha-ssaarabhi-varshinee

39.

[104]She manifests as devotee ascends further clearly,
[105]Removing obstacles assisting the rise* finally,
[106]She manifests in meditation as he rises past truly,
[107]With Her yogi unites - experieinces pure bliss finally.
- 52 -

Shloka 40.

तटिल्लतासमरुचि: षट्कच्रोपरि संस्थिता
महासक्ती: कुण्डलिनी बिससन्तुतनीयसी ॥४०

Tatillatha-sam-ruchih Shal-chakra-upari-sam-st'thithaa
Maha-aasakthih Kundalinee Bisa-thanthu-thaneeyasee

40.

[108]She seen as lightning, who impurities rinsed be,
[109]She who seated above the six *chakras* be,
[110]She obsessed in union of the devotees,
Of their mind in mediation and bliss actually.
- 53 -

---

[104] आज्ञाचक्रान्तरालस्था *Aajnaa-chakra-antharaala-st'thaa*

[105] रुद्रग्रन्थिविभेदिनी *Rudra-grantthi-vibhaethinee; * to sahasraara chakra*

[106] सहस्रारांबुजारूढ़ा *Sahasrara-ambuja-aaroodhaa*

[107] सुधासाराभिवर्षिणी *Sudha-saarabhi-varshinee*

[108] तटिल्लतासमरुचि: *Tatilatha-sam-ruchi*

[109] षट्कच्रोपरिसंस्थिता *Shal-chakra-upari-sam-st'thithaa*

[110] महासक्ती: *Maha-sakthih*

---

¹¹¹She who in the normal human being does be,
Asleep in the form of a snake and unknown truly.
¹¹²She as fine as thread inside stalk of lotus be,
She who unknown to human being ordinary.
- 54 -

Shloka 41.

भवानी भावनागम्या भवारण्यकुठारिका
भद्रप्रिया भद्रमूर्त्तिः भक्तसौभाग्यदायिनी ॥४१

Bhavaanee Bhaavana-agamya Bhava-aaranya-kut'taarika
Bhadra-priya Bhadra-moorthi Bhakta-soubhaagya-daayini

41.

¹¹³She the reality of all in material world be,
¹¹⁴She who is not understood by thought truly,
¹¹⁵She the axe which cut effects of wants surely,
Which keeps rising and tough to destroy be.
- 55 -

¹¹⁶She to whom all that is worthy, is dear clearly,
¹¹⁷She the manifest form of glorious and worthy,
Of meditation, surrender, mind and heart purity,
¹¹⁸She who gives of all fortunes to her devotee.
- 56 -

---

¹¹¹ कुण्डलिनी *Kundalinee*
¹¹² बिससन्तुतनीयसी *Bisa-thanthu-thaneeyasee*
¹¹³ भवानी *Bhavaanee*
¹¹⁴ भावनागम्या *Bhaavana-agamya*
¹¹⁵ भवारण्यकुठारिका *Bhava-aaranya-kut'taarikaa*
¹¹⁶ भद्रप्रिया *Bhadra-priya*
¹¹⁷ भद्रमूर्त्तिः *Bhadra-moorthy*
¹¹⁸ भक्तसौभाग्यदायिनी *Bhakta-soubhaagya-daayini*

Shloka 42.

भक्तिप्रिया भक्तिगम्या भक्तिवश्या भयापहा
शांभवी शारदाराध्या शर्व्वाणी शर्म्मदायिनी ॥४२

Bhakti-priyaa Bhakti-gamyaa Bakthi-vashyaa Bhaya-apahaa
Shaambhavee Sharada-aaradhyaa Sharvaanee Sharma-daayinee

42.

[119]She fond of devotion and dear to devotee be,
To none She has special love or hatred truly,
Who worship devotedly in Her, She in them be,
[120]She who is reached through devotion only.
- 57 -

[121]She be influenced through devotion only,
[122]She who destroys all fears in the devotee,
[123]She who bestows well being in the devotee,
[124]She worshipped by knowledgeable saintly.
- 58 -

Great and worthy worship and near to Her be,
[125]She who has manifested as the earth clearly,
[126]She who bestows happiness as peace truly,
In heart of devotee and bestores wealth really.
- 59 -

---

[119] भक्तिप्रिया *Bhakti-priya*

[120] भक्तिगम्या *Bhakti-gamyaa*

[121] भक्तिवश्या *Bhakti-vashyaa*

[122] भयापहा *Bhaya-apahaa*

[123] शांभवी *Shaambhavee*

[124] शारदाराध्या *Shaarada-aaradhya*

[125] शर्व्वाणी *Sharvaanee*

[126] शर्म्मदायिनी *Sharma-daayinee*

Shloka 43.

शाङ्करी श्रीकरी साध्वी शरच्चन्द्रनिभानना
शातोदरी शान्तिमती निराधारा निरञ्जना ॥४३

Shaam-karee Shree-karee Saadhwee Shara-chandra-nibha-aananaa
Shaado-o-udaree Shaanthi-mathee Ni-r-aadhaaraa Ni-r-anjanaa

43.

[127]She who gives happiness, well-being - Glory
[128]She who gives and source of all glories be,
[129]She most saintly, known by most saintly only,
Who not swayed by anything or anyone evil truly.
- 60 -

[130]She with the beauty of moon during Sharad be,
[131]She the daughter of mountain with caves be,
[132]She manifests as peace in heart of devotee,
[133]She independent of anything or anyone be.
- 61 -

Who aware of self as divine see Her in Self truly,
The unpure in heart - unable to see Her surely,
She untouched or uninfluenced by anything be,
[134]She manifests in heart of surrendered devotee.
- 62 -

---

[127] शाङ्करी *Shaam-karee*

[128] श्रीकरी *Sree-karee*

[129] साध्वी *Saadhwee*

[130] शरच्चन्द्रनिभानना *Shara-chandra-nibha-aananaa*

[131] शातोदरी *Shaada-o-udaree*

[132] शान्तिमती *Shaanthi-mathee*

[133] निराधारा *Ni-r-aadhaaraa*

[134] निरञ्जना *Ni-r-anjanaa*

Shloka 44.

निर्ल्लेपा निर्म्मला नित्या निराकारा निराकुला
निर्गुणा नीष्कला शान्ता निष्कामा निरुपप्लवा ॥४४

Ni-r-laepaa Nirmalaa Nithya Ni-r-aakaaraa Ni-r-aakulaa
Ni-r-gunaa Nish-kalaa Shaanthaa Nish-kaamaa Ni-r-upaplavaa

44.

[135]She who unbonded by effects of actions be,
[136]She who untainted by any impurities – Glory,
[137]She who pure awareness, eternal be – Glory,
[138]She who with no manifest form be – Glory.
- 63 -

[139]She who with no anxieties ever be – Glory,
[140]She beyond the three natural qualities* be,
[141]She not seen, heard, felt, known* actually,
She in devotee's heart who realises Self truly.
- 64 -

[142]She ever in balance, never perturbed be,
She manifests in them whose mind balance be,
[143]She who holds no desires to Her all glory,
[144]She who un-destroyable does be – all glory.
- 65 -

---

[135] निर्ल्लेपा *Ni-r-laepaa*

[136] निर्म्मला *Nirmalaa*

[137] नित्या *Nithya*

[138] निराकारा *Ni-r-aakaaraa*

[139] निराकुला *Ni-r-aakulaa*

[140] निर्गुणा *Ni-r-gunaa*; * of satwa, rajas and tamas; unknown by mind, sight or hearing

[141] नीष्कला *Nish-kalaa*; * by mind or sense

[142] शान्ता *Shaanthaa*

[143] निष्कामा *Nish-kaamaa*

[144] निरुपप्लवा *Ni-r-upaplavaa*

Shloka 45.

नित्यमुक्ता निर्विकारा निष्प्रपञ्चा निराश्रया
नित्यशुद्धा नित्यबुद्धा निरवद्या निरन्तरा ॥४५

Nithya-muktaa Ni-r-vikaaraa Nish-pra-panchaa Ni-r-aashrayaa
Nithya-shudhaa Nithya-budhhaa Ni-r-avadyaa Ni-r-antharaa

45.

[145]She who is free from everything worldly,
Who gives devotee freedom karma clearly,
[146]She who without change be ever infinitly,
[147]She who not from five basic elements* be.
- 66 -
[148]She who not dependant on anything be,
[149]She who untainted from any impurity be,
[150]She supreme knowledge, [151]worship worthy,
[152]She fills entire universe without a gap truly.
- 67 -

---

[145] नित्यमुक्ता *Nithya-muktaa*

[146] निर्विकारा *Ni-r-vikaaraa*

[147] निष्प्रपञ्चा *Nish-pra-panchaa;* * space, air, fire, water and earth

[148] निराश्रया *Ni-r-aashrayaa*

[149] नित्यशुद्धा *Nithya-shudhaa*

[150] नित्यबुद्धा *Nithya-budhaa*

[151] निरवद्या *Ni-r-avadyaa*

[152] निरन्तरा *Ni-r-antharaa*

Shloka 46.

निष्कारणा निष्कलङ्गा निरुपादिर्निरीश्वरा
नीरागा रागमथना निर्म्मदा मदनाशिनी ॥४६

Nish-kaaranaa Nish-kalangaa Ni-r-upaadi-r-ni-r-eeswaraa
Nee-raagaa Raaga-mat'thanaa Ni-r-madaa Mada-naashinee

46.

[153]She does not have a separate cause to be
[154]She who is free from all impurities – Glory,
She frees devotee from sin, ignorance fully,
[155]She who is free from illusions – all Glory.
- 68 -

[156]She does not have, or need protector truly,
[157]She who is unattached to all certainly,
She freedom from attachments for devotee,
[158]She gives freedom from attachments worldly.
- 69 -

Churns attachments, gets non-attachment truly,
[159]She has no illusions of pride in spite of glories,
[160]She destroys all illusions of self pride in devotee,
*She engulfs inferior desires in heart of devotee.
- 70 -

---

[153] निष्कारणा Nish-kaaranaa

[154] निष्कलङ्गा Nish-kalangaa

[155] निरुपादि Ni-r-upaadi

[156] निरीश्वरा Ni-r-eeswaraa

[157] नीरागा Nee-raagaa

[158] रागमथना Raaga-mat'thanaa

[159] निर्म्मदा Ni-r-madaa

[160] मदनाशिनी Mada-naashinee; * Also मदनः अशिनी Madana-asinee

---

Shloka 47.

निश्चिन्ता निरहंकारा निर्म्मोहा मोहनाशिनी
निर्म्मेमा ममताहन्त्री निष्पापा पापनाशिनी॥४७

Ni-s-chintha Ni-r-ahan-kaara Ni-r-moehaa Moeha-naashinee
Ni-r-mamaa Mamathaa-hanthree Nish-paapaa Paapa-naashinee

47.

[161]She unperturbed by thoughts and anxieties.
[162]She without pride acheives everything clearly,
[163]She who without illusions about anything be,
[164]She frees devotee from illusions certainly.

- 71 -

[165]She free of attachment to anything – Glory,
[166]She gives freeedom from possession fully,
[167]She untouched by sin due to untruth – Glory.
[168]She frees from sin's effects and impurities.

- 72 -

---

[161] *निश्चिन्ता Ni-s-chintha*

[162] *निरहंकारा Ni-r-ahan-kaara*

[163] *निर्म्मोहा Ni-r-moehaa*

[164] *मोहनाशिनी Moeha-naashinee*

[165] *निर्म्मेमा Ni-r-mamaa*

[166] *ममताहन्त्री Mamatha-hanthree*

[167] *निष्पापा Nish-paapaa*

[168] *पापनाशिनी Paapa-naashinee*

Shloka 48.

निष्क्रोधा क्रोधशमनी निर्लोभा लोभनाशिनी
निस्संशया संशयघ्नी निर्भवा भवनाशिनी ॥४८

Nish-kroedhaa Kroedha-shamanee Ni-r-loebhaa Loebha-naashinee
Ni-s-samshayaa Samshaya-ghni Ni-r-bhavaa Bhava-naashine

48.

[169]She free from anger and desire be – Glory,
[170]She frees from anger the devotee – Glory,
[171]She who does not grab from others – Glory,
[172]She frees desire to grab from others – Glory.
- 73 -

[173]She is sure and can be trusted undoubtedly,
[174]She who frees from fears and doubts – Glory,
[175]She who does not have an origin – Glory,
[176]She who frees from all things worldly* - Glory.
- 74 -

---

[169] निष्क्रोधा Nish-kroedhaa

[170] क्रोधशमनी Kroedha-shamanee

[171] निर्लोभा Ni-r-loebhaa

[172] लोभनाशिनी Loebha-naashinee

[173] निस्संशया Ni-s-samshayaa

[174] संशयघ्नी Samshaya-ghni

[175] निर्भवा Ni-r-bhavaa

[176] भवनाशिनी Bhava-naashine; * pains and sorrows

श्री ललिता सहस्रनाम

Shloka 49.

निर्विकल्पा निराबाधा निर्भेदा भेदनाशिनी
निन्नाशा मृत्युमथनी निष्क्रिया निष्परिग्रहा ॥४९

Ni-r-vikalpaa Ni-r-aabaadhaa Ni-r-bhaeda Bhaeda-naashinee
Ni-r-naashaa Mr'thyu-matthanee Nish-kriyaa Nish-pari-grahaa

49.

[177]She supreme truth, knowledge only be,
[178]She unaffected by illusions be – Glory,
[179]She to whom everything same be – Glory,
She not different or separate from truth be.
- 75 -

[180]She destroys feeling of separateness – Glory,
[181]She who undestroyable does be – Glory,

[182]She who can destroy death totally – Glory,
She frees from birth and death cycle – Glory.
- 76 -

[183]She who has nothing to do – all Glory,
She helps do nothing, even if senses* be,
She helps to be unattached to actions – Glory,
[184]She requires nothing obviously – Glory.
- 77 -

---

[177] निर्विकल्पा Ni-r-vikalpaa

[178] निराबाधा Ni-r-aabaadhaa

[179] निर्भेदा Ni-r-bhaedaa

[180] भेदनाशिनी Bhaeda-naashinee

[181] निन्नाशा Ni-r-naashaa

[182] मृत्युमथनी Mr'thyu-mat'thanee

[183] निष्क्रिया Nish-kriyaa; *in their functions as eyes see, ears hear etc.

[184] निष्परिग्रहा Nish-pari-grahaa

Shloka 50.

निस्तुला नीलचिकुरा निरपाया निरत्यया
दुर्ल्लभा दुर्ग्गमा दुर्ग्गा दुखहन्त्री सुखप्रदा ॥५०

Ni-s-thulaa Neela-chikuraa Ni-r-apaayaa Nir-athyayaa
Du-r-labhaa Du-r-gamaa Du-r-gaa Dukha-hanthree Sukha-pradaa

50.

[185]She who with no comparision be – Glory,
[186]Her dark, deep blue hair most beautiful be,
[187]She who with no fear of anything – Glory,
She who frees from fears of any kind – Glory.
- 78 -

[188]She who cannot be got across to – Glory,
She breaks no rules set by herself – Glory,
She protects from all fears and cares – Glory,
[189]She extrememly difficult to achieve – Glory.
- 79 -

She is reached only by the most saintly,
[190]She can not be neared easily – Glory,
[191]She who the nine Durga does be – Glory,
She destroys the evil in mind – Glory.
- 80 -

---

[185] निस्तुला Ni-s-thulaa

[186] नीलचिकुरा Neela-chikuraa

[187] निरपाया Ni-r-apaayaa

[188] निरत्यया Nir-athyayaa

[189] दुर्ल्लभा Du-r-labhaa

[190] दुर्ग्गमा Du-r-gamaa

[191] दुर्ग्गा Du-r-gaa

She helps cross problems of life – Glory,
Which are so difficult to cross – Glory,
[192]She who can destroy all sorrows – Glory,
[193]She gives happiness and pleasure – Glory.
- 81 -

Shloka 51.

दुष्टदूरा दूराचारशमनी दोषवर्जिता
सर्वज्ञा सान्द्रकरुणा समानधिकवर्जिता ॥५१

*Dushta-dooraa Du-r-aachaara-shamanee Dosha-varjithaa
Sarva-jnaa Sandra-karunaa Samaana-adhika-varjjithaa*

51.

[194]She is very far to the evil ones – Glory,
She the evil can never but reach – Glory,
She keeps evil away from devotees – Glory,
[195]She who destroys evil practices – Glory.
- 82 -

[196]She does not have any faults – Glory,
[197]She who knows everything – Glory,
[198]She full of kindness mercy be – Glory,
[199]She who is incomparable – Glory.
- 83 -

---

[192] दुखहन्त्री *Dukha-hanthree*

[193] सुखप्रदा *Sukha-pradaa*

[194] दुष्टदूरा *Dushta-dooraa*

[195] दूराचारशमनी *Du-r-aachaara-shamanee*

[196] दोषवर्जिता *Dosha-varjithaa*

[197] सर्वज्ञा *Sarva-jnaa*

[198] सान्द्रकरुणा *Saandra-karunaa*

[199] समानधिकवर्जिता *Samaana-adhika-varjjithaa*

Shloka 52.

सर्वशक्तिमयी सर्वमंगला सत्गतिप्रदा
सर्वेश्वरी सर्वमयी सर्वमन्त्रस्वरूपिणी॥५२

Sarva-shakti-mayee Sarva-mangalaa Sath-gathi-pradaa
Sarva-eswaree Sarva-mayee Sarva-manthra-swaroopinee

52.

[200]She personification of all energy – Glory,
[201]She personification of all good be – Glory,
She who grants all glories to the devotee,
[202]She frees from births and deaths – Glory.
- 84 -

She the shelter for saintly ones be – Glory,
[203] She who goddess of all does be – Glory,
[204]She fills everything in universe – Glory,
[205]She epitome of all manthras be – Glory.
- 85 -

---

[200] सर्वशक्तिमयी Sarva-shakti-mayee

[201] सर्वमंगला Sarva-mangalaa

[202] सत्गतिप्रदा Sath-gathi-pradaa

[203] सर्वेश्वरी Sarva-eswaree

[204] सर्वमयी Sarva-mayee

[205] सर्वमन्त्रस्वरूपिणी Sarva-manthra-swaroopinee

3rd Shathaka

Shloka 53.

सर्व्वयन्त्रात्मिका सर्व्वतन्त्ररूपा मनोन्मनी
माहेश्वरी महादेवी महालक्ष्मीर्मृडप्रिया॥५३

*Sarva-yanthra-aathmikaa Sarva-thanthra-roopaa Mana-o-unmanee
Maha-esware Maha-devee Maha-lakshmee-r-mr'da-priyaa*

53.

[206]She who represented by all yantras* – Glory,
[207]She who manifests as all thanthras – Glory,
[208]She manifests at time of full surrender – Glory,
[209]She the great lord of the universe – Glory.

- 86 -

She the consort of *Maheswar** does be – Glory,
[210]Her physical body great universe be – Glory,
[211] She the goddess of wealth does be – Glory,
[212]She very dear to Lord Shiv does be – Glory.

- 87 -

---

[206] सर्व्वयन्त्रात्मिका *Sarva-yanthra-aathmikaa; * Talisman*

[207] सर्व्वतन्त्ररूपा *Sarva-thanthra-roopaa*

[208] मनोन्मनी *Mana-o-unmanee*

[209] माहेश्वरी *Maha-eswaree; *Lord Of Universe*

[210] महादेवी *Maha-devee; * God of all gods*

[211] महालक्ष्मी *Maha-lakshmee*

[212] मृडप्रिया *Mr'da-priyaa*

Shloka 54.

महारूपा महापूज्या महापातकनाशिनी
महामाया महासत्वा महाशक्तिर्महारतिः ॥५४

Maha-roopaa Maha-poojyaa Maha-paathake-naashinee
Maha-maayaa Maha-sathwaa Maha-shakti-r-maha-rathih

54.

[213]She who with the greatest form be – Glory,
She who the indestructible truth be – Glory,
[214]She worshipped by the learned – Glory,
[215]She destroys sin knowingly or unknowingly.
- 88 -

[216]She who is the greatest illusions – Glory,
[217]She has great sainlty qualities* – Glory,
[218]She who with greatest strength be – Glory,
[219]She happiness, satisfaction be – Glory.
- 89 -

---

[213] *महारूपा* Maha-roopaa

[214] *महापूज्या* Maha-poojyaa

[215] *महापातकनाशिनी* Maha-paathaka-naashinee

[216] *महामाया* Maha-maayaa

[217] *महासत्वा* Maha-sat'thwaa; * strength, intelligence, purity

[218] *महाशक्तिः* Maha-shaktih

[219] *महारतिः* Maha-rathih

Shloka 55.

महाभोगा महैश्वर्या महावीर्या महाबला
महाबुद्धिर्महासिद्धिः महायोगेश्वरेश्वरी ॥५५॥

Maha-boegaa Maha-aishwayaraa maha-veeryaa Maha-balaa
Maha-budhi-r-maha-sidhi Maha-yogeswara-eeswari

55.

[220] She who enjoys great pleasures – Glory,
[221] She who has the greatest wealth – Glory,
[222] She who has the greatest valour – Glory,
[223] She who is the very strongest – Glory.

- 90 -

[224]She the great intelligect does be – Glory,
Who manifests as intelligence in living truly,
[225] She has great super natural powers – Glory,
[226] She who is goddess of great yogis – Glory.

- 91 -

---

[220] महाभोगा *Maha-boegaa*

[221] महैश्वर्या *Maha-aishwayaraa*

[222] महावीर्या *Maha-veeryaa*

[223] महाबला *Maha-balaa*

[224] महाबुद्धिः *Maha-budhih*

[225] महासिद्धिः *Maha-sidhih*

[226] महायोगेश्वरेश्वरी *Maha-yogeswara-eeswari*

Shloka 56.

महा तन्त्रा महामन्त्रा महायन्त्रा महासना
महायागक्रमाराध्या महाभैरवपूजिता ॥५६

Maha-tanthraa maha-mantraa Maha-yanthraa Maha-aasanaa
Maha-yaaga-krama-aaraadhya Maha-bhairava-poojithaa

56.

[227]She has the greatest Thantra sasthras – Glory,
[228]She who has the greatest manthras – Glory,
[229]She who has the greatest yanthras – Glory,
[230]She who seated in supreme truth be – Glory.
- 92 -

She the real Truth undoubtedly be – Glory,
[231]She worshipped by great sacrifices orderly,
[232]She worshipped by great Bhairava be – Glory,
By 'Time' that destroys all the creation finally.
- 93 -

---

[227] महातन्त्रा Maha-tanthraa

[228] महामन्त्रा Maha-mantraa

[229] महायन्त्रा Maha-yanthraa

[230] महासना Maha-aasanaa

[231] महायागक्रमाराध्या Maha-yaaga-krama-aaraadhya

[232] महाभैरवपूजिता Maha-bhairava-poojithaa

Shloka 57.

महेश्वरमहाकल्पमहाताण्डवसाक्षिणी

महाकामेशमहिषी महात्रिपुरसुन्दरी ॥५७

Maha-eswara-maha-kalpa-maha-thaandava-saakshinee
Maha-kaamesa-mahishee Mah-tri-pura-sundaree

57.

[233]She sole witness to the great celebration be,
After universe dissolves into the truth finally,
Great queen to them who controls wants fully,
She who frees the devotee from all desires fully.
- 94 -

[234]The great queen of knowledgeable ones be,
in whom desire, mind, senses sublimed do be,
She the consort of great Kameshwara – Glory,
[235]Most beautiful – ruling all three realms – Glory.
- 95 -

---

[233] *महेश्वरमहाकल्पमहाताण्डवसाक्षिणी* Maha-eswara-maha-kalpa-maha-thaandava-saakshinee

[234] *महाकामेशमहिषी* Maha-kaama-esa-mahishee

[235] *महात्रिपुरसुन्दरी* Mah-tri-pura-sundar () the physical body which exists during the life span, () the life which leaves the physical body at the time of death and () the cause of life taking on another physical body viz. the effects of all karma s

Shloka 58.

चतुषष्टियुपचाराढ्या चतु:षष्टिकलामयी
महाचतुषष्टिकोटियोगिनीगणसेविता ॥५८

Chathu-shashti-upachaara-aadhyaa Chathu-shashti-kala-mayee
Maha-chathu-shashti-koedi-yoginee-gana-saevithaa

58.

[236]She worshipped through disciplines – Glory,
[237]She manifested as the forms of art – Glory,
[238]She served by the knowledgeable – Glory,
Who in union with the divine do be – Glory.
- 96 -

Shloka 59.

मनुविद्या चन्द्रविद्या चन्द्रमण्डलमद्ध्यगा
चारुरूपा चारुहासा चारुचन्द्रकलाधरा ॥५९

Manu-vidyaa Chandra-vidyaa Chandra-mandala-madhya-gaa
Chaaru-roopa Chaaru-haasaa Chaaru-chandra-kala-dharaa

59.

[239] She Sri Vidya expounded by Manu be - Glory,
[240] She Sri Vidya as expounded by Moon – Glory,
[241]She reched by mediation and awakening be,
She center of universe of the moon – Glory.
- 97 -

---

[236] चतुषष्टियुपचाराढ्या Chathu-shashti-upachaara-aadhyaa
[237] चतु:षष्टिकलामयी Chathu-shashti-kala-mayee
[238] महाचतुषष्टिकोटियोगिनीगणसेविता Maha-chathu-shashti-koedi-yoginee-gana-saevithaa
[239] मनुविद्या Manu-vidyaa
[240] चन्द्रविद्या Chandra-vidyaa
[241] चन्द्रमण्डलमद्ध्यगा Chandra-mandala-madhya-gaa

---

[242] She who the most beautiful surely be – Glory,
She who manifests as the beauty of all – Glory,
[243] She has a beautiful smile certainly – Glory,
[244]She adorned by the beautiful moon – Glory.
- 98 -

Shloka 60.

चराचरजगन्नाथा चक्रराजनिकेतना
पार्व्वती पद्मनयना पद्मरागसमप्रभा ॥६०

*Chara-achara-jagath-naat'thaa Chakra-raaja-nikethana
Paarvathi Padma-nayana Padma-raaaga-sama-prabhaa*

60.

[245]She lord of all moving, immobile be – Glory,
[246]She worshiped in middle of Shri Chakra be,
She who is the life of the living being – Glory,
[247]She daughter of the mountains be – Glory.
- 99 -

[248]Her eyes as untouched lotus petals be – Glory,
Untouched by impurities of the world – Glory,
Untouched by the water in which it stays,
[249]She shines as the *Padma-raga* gem – Glory.
- 100 -

---

[242] चारुरूपा Chaaru-roopa

[243] चारुहासा Chaaru-haasaa

[244] चारुचन्द्रकलाधरा Chaaru-chandra-kala-dharaa

[245] चराचरजगन्नाथा Chara-achara-jagath-naat'thaa

[246] चक्रराजनिकेतना Chakra-raaja-nikethana

[247] पार्व्वती Paarvathi

[248] पद्मनयना Padma-nayana

[249] पद्मरागसमप्रभा Padma-raaaga-sama-prabhaa

Shloka 61.

पञ्चप्रेतासनासीना पञ्चब्रह्मस्वरूपिणी
चिन्मयी परमानन्दा विज्ञानघनरूपिणी ॥६१॥

Pancha-praetha-aasana-aaseena Pancha-brahma-swaroopini
Chinmayee Param-aananda Vijnaana-ghana-roopini

61.

[250]She five elements space, air, fire, water earth be,
She sits on the seat of five bodies* – Glory,
[251] She personification of five brahmas* – Glory,
She manifested as the five organs – Glory.
- 101 -

[252]She who is the life* in the living – Glory,
[253]She the supreme truth and happiness – Glory,
[254]She who pure knowledge does be – Glory,
She knowledge based on science be – Glory.
- 102 -

---

[250] पञ्चप्रेतासनासीना *Pancha-praetha-aasana-aaseena* ; *Brahma, Vishnu, Rudra, Eesa, Sadasiva

[251] पञ्चब्रह्मस्वरूपिणी *Pancha-brahma-swaroopini*; *Brahma, Vishnu, Rudra, Eesa and Sadasiva with their Shakthi

[252] चिन्मयी *Chinmayee*; *chit

[253] परमानन्दा *Param-aanandaa*

[254] विज्ञानघनरूपिणी *Vijnaana-ghana-roopini*

Shloka 62.

ध्यानध्यातृध्येयरूपा धर्म्माधर्म्मविवर्जिता
विश्वरूपा जागरिणी स्वपन्ती तैजसात्मिका ॥६२

Dhyaana-dyaath'r-dhyaeya-roopaa Dharma-adharma-vivarjjitaa
Vishwa-roopaa Jaagarinee Swapanthee Thaijas-aatmikaa

62.

[255]She meditation, meditator and its process be,
[256]She beyond justice and in-justice – Glory,
[257]She who manifested as universe – Glory,
[258]She as awareness in the living be – Glory.
- 103 -

She makes senses aware of world – Glory,
[259]She manifests as state of dream – Glory,
She who always awake does be – Glory,
[260]She life that experiences dream – Glory,
- 104 -

---

[255] ध्यानध्यातृध्येयरूपा *Dhyaana-dyaath'r-dhyaeya-roopaa*

[256] धर्म्माधर्म्मविवर्जिता *Dharma-adharma-vivarjjitaa*

[257] विश्वरूपा *Vishwa-roopaa*

[258] जागरिणी *Jaagarinee*

[259] स्वपन्ती *Swapanthee*

[260] तैजसात्मिका *Thaijas-aatmikaa*

Shloka 63.

सुप्ता प्राज्ञात्मिका तुर्या सर्वावस्थाविवर्जिता
सृष्टिकर्त्री ब्रह्मरूपा गोप्त्री गोविन्दरूपिणी ॥६३

Supthaa Praajnaa-aathmika Thuryaa Sarva-avast'tha-vivarjithaa
Sr'shti-karthree Brahma-roopa Goepthree Govinda-roopinee

63.

[261]She who in deep sleep does be – Glory,
[262]She who yet awakened does be – Glory,
[263]She who exists in stage of trance – Glory,
[264]She who is beyond even these states – Glory,
- 105 -

[265]She all in universe and universe be – Glory,
[266]She the form of the supreme truth – Glory,
[267]She who protects the full universe – Glory,
[268]She who but all the vedas does be – Glory.
- 106 -

---

[261] सुप्ता *Supthaa*

[262] प्राज्ञात्मिका *Praajnaa-aathmika*

[263] तुर्या *Thuryaa*

[264] सर्वावस्थाविवर्जिता *Sarva-avast'tha-vivarjithaa*

[265] सृष्टिकर्त्री *Sr'shti-karthree*

[266] ब्रह्मरूपा *Brahma-roopa*

[267] गोप्त्री *Goepthree*

[268] गोविन्दरूपिणी *Govinda-roopinee*

Shloka 64.

संहारिणी रुद्ररूपा तिरोधानकरीश्वरी
सदाशिवाऽनुग्रहदा पञ्चकृत्यपरायणा ॥६४॥

Samhaarinee Rudra-roopa Thirodaana-karee-eeswaree
Sada-shiva-anugraha-daa pancha-kr'thya-paraayanaa

64.

[269]She who destroys everything – Glory,
[270]She destruction of all things be – Glory,
[271]Into Herself all merge finally – Glory,
[272]The lord of everything does be – Glory,
- 107 -

[273]She who is forever the source of glories,
She who gives glories to her true devotee,
[274]She who showers blessings on devotees,
[275]She alters all to five basic elements* lastly.
- 108 -

---

[269] संहारिणी *Samhaarinee*

[270] रुद्ररूपा *Rudra-roopa*

[271] तिरोधानकरी *Thirodhaana-karee*

[272] ईश्वरी *Eeswaree*

[273] सदाशिवा *Sada-shiva*

[274] अनुग्रहदा *Anugraha-daa*

[275] पञ्चकृत्यपरायणा *pancha-kr'thya-paraayanaa; *space, air, fire, water and earth*

Shloka 65.

भानुमण्डलमद्ध्यस्था भैरवी भगमालिनी
पद्मासना भगवती पद्मनाभसहोदरी ॥६५

Bhaanu-mandala-madhya-st'thaa Bhairavee Bhaga-maalinee
Padma-aasana Bhagavathee Padma-naabha-sahodaree

65.

[276]She source of sun's illumination – Glory,
[277]She destroyer of the universe – Glory,
She the consort of Bhairav be – Glory,
[278]She adorned by garland of six qualities*.
- 109 -

[279]She whose seat a lotus does be – Glory,
Untouched, uninfluenced by anything truly,
[280]She protects those who worship sincerely,
[281]She in whom potential to create – Glory.
- 110 -

---

[276] भानुमण्डलमद्ध्यस्था *Bhaanu-mandala-madhya-st'thaa*

[277] भैरवी *Bhairavee*

[278] भगमालिनी *Bhaga-maalinee; * glories, wealth, fame, knowledge, non-attachment, truth*

[279] पद्मासना *Padma-aasana lotus pose*

[280] भगवती *Bhagavathee*

[281] पद्मनाभसहोदरी *Padma-naabha-saha-o-udaree*

श्री ललिता सहस्रनाम

Shloka 66.

उन्मेषनिमिषोल्पन्नविपन्नभुवनावली
सहस्रशीर्षवदना सहस्राक्षी सहस्रपात् ॥६६॥

Unmaesha-nimisha-o-ulpanna-vipanna-bhuvana-aavalee
Sahasra-sheersha-vadanaa Sahasra-akshee Sahasra-paath

66.

[282]She creates, destroys by eye lids effort truly,
[283]She has thousands of faces, heads – Glory,
[284]She who has thousands of eyes – Glory,
[285]She who has thousands of feet – Glory.

- 111 -

Shloka 67.

आब्रह्मकीटजननी वर्णाश्रमविधायिनी
निजाज्ञारूपनिगमा पुण्यापुण्यफलप्रदा ॥६७॥

Aabrahma-keeta-jananee Varna-aashrama-vidhaayinee
Nija-aajnaa-roopa-nigamaa Puniya-apuniya-ppala-pradaa

67.

[286] She the origin of all beings* does be – Glory,
[287] She created four division of society – Glory,
[288]She as the vedas guides the devotee – Glory,
[289]She who grant fruits for evil and the saintly.

- 112 -

---

[282] उन्मेषनिमिषोल्पन्नविपन्नभुवनावली Unmaesha-nimisha-o-ulpanna-vipanna-bhuvana-aavalee

[283] सहस्रशीर्षवदना Sahasra-sheersha-vadanaa

[284] सहस्राक्षी Sahasra-akshee

[285] सहस्रपात् Sahasra-paath

[286] आब्रह्मकीटजननी Aa-brahma-keeta-jananee; * from worm to Lord Brahma

[287] वर्णाश्रमविधायिनी Varna-aashrama-vidhaayinee

[288] निजाज्ञारूपनिगमा Nija-aajnaa-roopa-nigamaa

[289] पुण्यापुण्यफलप्रदा Puniya-apuniya-ppala-pradaa

Shloka 68.

श्रुतिसीमन्तसिन्दूरीकृतपादाब्जधूलिका
सकलागमसन्दोहशुक्तिसंपुटमौक्तिका ॥६८

Sruthi-seemantha-sindooree-kr'tha-paada-abja-dhoolikaa
Sakala-aagama-sandoha-shukti-sampuda-mouktikaa

68.

[290]Dust of Her feet essence of Upanishads be,
Sindhoora in hair parting of Vedic mother be,
[291]She the nose ring the pearl in the oysters be,
The pearl holding shell of the Vedas – Glory.

- 113 -

Shloka 69.

पुरुषार्थप्रदा पूर्णा भोगिनी भुवनेश्वरी
अंबिकाऽनादिनिधना हरिब्रह्मेन्द्रसेविता ॥६९

Purusha-aart'tha-pradaa Poornaa Bhoeginee Bhuvana-eswaree
Ambikaa An-aadi-nidhanaa Hari-brahma-e-indra-saevithaa

69.

[292]She grants four needs* of human being – Glory,
[293]She is always complete unaffectedly – Glory,
[294]She who enjoys universe and all in it – Glory,
She receives all offered by the true devotee.

- 114 -

---

[290] श्रुतिसीमन्तसिन्दूरीकृतपादाब्जधूलिका

[291] सकलागमसन्दोहशुक्तिसंपुटमौक्तिका *Sakala-aagama-sandoeha-shukti-sampuda-moukthikaa*

[292] पुरुषार्थप्रदा *Purusha-aart'tha-pradaa*; * *righteousness, wealth, desires and liberation from the cycle of birth and death*

[293] पूर्णा *Poornaa*

[294] भोगिनी *Bhoeginee*

[295]The lord of the entire universe – Glory,
[296]The mother of the entire universe – Glory,
[297]She without a beginning or end – Glory,
[298]She worshipped by worthy in universe be.

- 115 -

Shloka 70.

नारायणी नादरूपा नामरूपविवर्जिता
ह्रीङ्कारी ह्रीमती हर्द्या हेयोपादेयवर्जिता ॥७०

Naaraayanee Naada-roopa Naama-roopa-vivarjithaa
Hreem-kaare Hree-mathee Hr'dyaa Haeya-o-upaadeya-varjjithaa

70.

[299]She exists in water which part of life be,
[300]She the shape of music, sound – Glory,
[301]She undefined by any name or form be,
She who without a name or a form – Glory.

- 116 -

[302]She creates shame in adverse activities,
[303]She who extremely shy does be – Glory,
[304]She who exists in heart of the devotee,
[305]With no aspect accepted or rejected clearly.

- 117 -

---

[295] भुवनेश्वरी *Bhuvana-eswaree*

[296] अंबिका *Ambika*

[297] अनादिनिधना *An-aadi-nidhanaa*

[298] हरिब्रह्मेन्द्रसेविता *Hari-brahama-e-indra-saevithaaa*

[299] नारायणी *naaraayanee*

[300] नादरूपा *Naada-roopa*

[301] नामरूपविवर्जिता *Naama-roopa-vivarjithaa*

[302] ह्रीङ्कारी *Hreen-kaaree*

[303] ह्रीमती *Hreemathee*

[304] हर्द्या *Hr'dyaa*

[305] हेयोपादेयवर्जिता *Haeya-upaadaeya-varjithaa*

4ᵗʰ Shathaka

Shloka 71.

राजराजार्चिता राज्ञी रम्या राजीवलोचना
रञ्जिनी रमणी रस्या रणत्किडिणिमेखला ॥७१॥

Raja-raja-architha Raajnee Ramyaa Rajeeva-loechanaa
Ranjinee Remanee Rasyaa Ranal-kingini-maekhalaa

71.

[306]She queen of supreme truth – Glory,
With Her unlimited greatness – Glory,
She adored by King of kings – Glory,
[307]She queen of worlds, with great authority.
- 118 -

She the queen of Kameshwar – Glory,
[308]In Her, hearts of devotees are happily,
[309]Her eyes sees all but as lotus untouched be,
[310]She fills heart with much happiness – Glory.
- 119 -

She who plays with her devotees – Glory,
[311]She engages heart and fills it with joy fully.
[312]She who worth experiencing be – Glory.
[313]Dons golden waist band with bells – Glory.
- 120 -

---

[306] राजराजार्चिता Raja-raja-architha

[307] राज्ञी Raajnee

[308] रम्या Ramyaa

[309] राजीवलोचना Rajeeva-loechanaa

[310] रञ्जिनी Ranjinee

[311] रमणी Ramanee

[312] रस्या Rasyaa

[313] रणत्किडिणिमेखला Ranath kinkini mekhala

Shloka 72.

रमा राकेन्दुवदना रतिरूपा रतिप्रिया
रक्षाकरी राक्षसघ्नी रामा रमणलंपटा ॥७२

Rema Raaka-e-indu-vadanaa Rathi-roopa Rathi-priya
Rakshaa-karee Raakshasa-ghnee Raamaa Ramana-lampadaa

72.

[314]She worshipped as Lakshmi, Saraswathi
She is worshiped for wealth and glory,
[315]Her face as beautiful as the full moon be,
Manifests as everything that beautiful be.
- 121 -

[316]She who manifests as ecstacy – Glory,
[317]To Her ecstacy of yogi is dear – Glory,
[318]She who protects the world – Glory,
[319]She destroys evil in devotee – Glory.
- 122 -

[320]In Her saintly find happiness truly,
She who is the feminine – Glory,
[321]She loves, engages with devotee,
She intent in loving her lord – Glory.
- 123 -

---

[314] रमा *Rema*

[315] राकेन्दुवदना *Raaka-e-indu-vadanaa*

[316] रतिरूपा *Rathi-roopa*

[317] रतिप्रिया *Rathi-priya*

[318] रक्षाकरी *Rakshaa-karee*

[319] राक्षसघ्नी *Raakshasa-ghnee*

[320] रामा *Raamaa*

[321] रमणलंपटा *Ramana-lampadaa*

Shloka 73.

काम्या कामकलारूपा कदंबकुसुमप्रिया
कल्याणी जगतीकन्दा करुणाससागरा ॥७३

Kaamyaa Kaama-kala-roopa Kadamba-kusuma-priyaa
Kalyaanee Jagathee-kandaa Karunaa-rasa-saagaraa

73.

She who is desired universally – Glory,
[322]She desired and sought for by the saintly,
She who is of the form of love – Glory,
[323]She who takes form of desires clearly.
- 124 -

She the personification of art of love be,
She fond of flowers of the kadamba tree,
[324]She revered by offering of flowers surely,
[325]She who gives of glories to Her devotee.
- 125 -

[326]She who as root of the world does be,
[327]She full of kindness towards Her devotee,
She the sea of the juice of mercy – Glory,
She compassionate – To her salutation be.
- 126 -

---

[322] काम्या *Kaamyaa*

[323] कामकलारूपा *Kaama-kala-roopa*

[324] कदंबकुसुमप्रिया *Kadamba-kusuma-priyaa*

[325] कल्याणी *Kalyaanee*

[326] जगतीकन्दा *Jagathee-kandaa*

[327] करुणाससागरा *Karuna-rasa-saagaraa*

श्री ललिता सहस्रनाम

Shloka 74.

कलावती कालालापा कान्ता कादंबरीप्रिया
वरदा वामनयना वारुणीमदविह्वला ॥७४

Kalavathee Kala-aalaapa Kaanthaa Kaadambari-priya
Vara-daa Vaama-nayanaa Vaarunee-mada-vihualaa

74.

[328]She manifests as all forms of art – Glory,
[329]She worshipped through hymns – Glory,
She the divine hymns in praise – Glory,
[330]She glitters and extremely beautiful be.
- 127 -

[331]To Her devotees intoxicated with piety be,
[332]She gives devotee what worthy be – Glory,
[333]She who with most beautiful eyes – Glory,
[334]She drunk in supreme bliss, knowledge be.
- 128 -

---

[328] कलावती Kalavathee

[329] कालालापा Kala-aalaapa

[330] कान्ता Kaanthaa

[331] कादंबरीप्रिया Kaadambari-priya

[332] वरदा Vara-daa

[333] वामनयना Vaama-nayanaa

[334] वारुणीमदविह्वला Vaarunee-mada-vihualaa

Shloka 75.

वीश्वाधिका वेदवेद्या विन्ध्याचलनिवासिनी
वीधात्री वेदजननी विष्णुमाया विलासिनी ॥७५

Viswa-adhikaa Veda-vaedyaa Vindhya-achala-nivaasinee
Vidhathree Veda-jananee Vishnu-maaya Vilaasinee

75.

[335]She exists beyond the universe – Glory,
[336]Worthy of being known by vedas only,
[337]She stays on Vindhya mountains – Glory,
[338]She cares for the universe dedicatedly.
- 129 -

She who carries the universe – Glory,
[339]She who created the vedas – Glory,
[340]She who lives as Vishnu maya – Glory,
[341]She who enjoys love making – Glory.
- 130 -

---

[335] वीश्वाधिका *Viswa-adhikaa*

[336] वेदवेद्या *Veda-vaedyaa*

[337] विन्ध्याचलनिवासिनी *Vindhya-achala-nivaasinee*

[338] वीधात्री *Vidhathree*

[339] वेदजननी *Veda-jananee*

[340] विष्णुमाया *Vishnu-maaya*

[341] विलासिनी *Vilaasinee*

Shloka 76.

क्षेत्रस्वरूपा क्षेत्रेशी क्षेत्रक्षेत्रज्ञपालिनी
क्षयवृद्धिविनिर्म्मुक्ता क्षेत्रपालसमर्च्चिता ॥७६

Kshetra-swaroopa Kshetra-a-esee Kshetra-kshetra-jna-paalinee
Kshaya-vr'dhi-vi-ni-r-muktaa Kshetra-paala-sama-archithaa

76.

[342]She personification of the body – Glory,
[343]She lord of the physical body – Glory,
[344]She the being, life which keeps it truly,
[345]She neither decreases or increases surely.

 - 131 -

[346]She who worshipped by the life be,
That life which is in the being – Glory,
She who is worshipped by them be,
Who look after all the bodies – Glory.

 - 132 -

---

[342] क्षेत्रस्वरूपा *Kshetra-swaroopa*

[343] क्षेत्रेशी *Kshetra-a-esee*

[344] क्षेत्रक्षेत्रज्ञपालिनी *Kshetra-kshetra-jna-paalinee*

[345] क्षयवृद्धिविनिर्म्मुक्ता *Kshaya-vr'dhi-vi-ni-r-muktaa*

[346] क्षेत्रपालसमर्च्चिता *Kshetra-paala-sama-archithaa*

Sri Lalita Sahasranama

Shloka 77.

विजया विमला वन्द्या वन्दारुजनवल्सला
वाग्वादिनी वामकेशी वहिनमण्डलवासिनी ॥७७

Vijayaa Vimalaa Vandyaa Vandaaru-jana-valsalaa
Vaak-vaadinee Vaama-kaesi Vahni-mandala-vaasinee

77.

[347]She who is always victorious – Glory,
[348]She untainted by ignorance, illusion be,
She who is the pure awareness – Glory,
[349]She who is worth worshipping – Glory.
- 133 -

[350]She is extremely fond of Her devotees,
[351]She blesses with accurate vocabulary,
[352]She the lord of all human beings be,
[353]She the fire of universal life be – Glory.
- 134 -

---

[347] विजया *Vijayaa*

[348] विमला *Vimalaa*

[349] वन्द्या *Vandyaa*

[350] वन्दारुजनवल्सला *Vandaaru-jana-valsalaa*

[351] वाग्वादिनी *Vaak-vaadinee*

[352] वामकेशी *Vaamaka-eesi or Vaama-kaesi*

[353] वहिनमण्डलवासिनी *Vahni-mandala-vaasinee*

Shloka 78.

भक्तिमत्कल्पलतिका पशुपाशविमोचिनी
संहृताशेषपाषण्डा सदाचारप्रवर्त्तिका ॥७८

Bhaktimath-kalpa-lathikaa Pashu-paasha-vimoechinee
Samhr'tha-ashesha-paashandaa Sath-aachaara-pravartthikaa

78.

[354]She grants Her devotee their boon truly,
[355]She frees from karma* bondage surely,
She rids shackles from the living – Glory,
[356]She destroys who against scriptures be.
- 135 -

She ends them who leave their faith – Glory,
[357]She who engaged in only saintly activities,
She manifests as saintly activities in devotee,
She acts by good conduct clearly – Glory.
- 136 -

---

[354] भक्तिमत्कल्पलतिका *Bhaktimath-kalpa-lathikaa*

[355] पशुपाशविमोचिनी *Pashu-paasha-vimoechinee; * of effects of action*

[356] संहृताशेषपाषण्डा *Samhr'tha-ashesha-paashandaa*

[357] सदाचारप्रवर्त्तिका *Sath-aachaara-pravarthikaa*

Shloka 79.

तापत्रयाग्निसन्तप्तसमाह्लादनचन्द्रिका
तरुणी तापसाराध्या तनुमद्ध्या तमोपहा ॥७९

Thaapa-thraya-agni-santhaptha Sam-aahlaadana-chandrikaa
Tharunee Thaapasa-aaradhyaa Thanu-madhyaa Tama-o-apahaa

79.

[358]She as moonlight ever soothingly,
Those burning with heat agonies*,
[359]She youthful unaffected by time be,
[360]She worshipped by Sages saintly.
- 137 -

[361]She manifests as the present be,
She who has a narrow hip – Glory,
[362]She who removes darkness fully,
Who destroys ignorance – Glory.
- 138 -

---

[358] तापत्रयाग्निसन्तप्तसमाह्लादनचन्द्रिका *Thaapa-thraya-agni-santhaptha Sam-aahlaadana-chandrikaa*; *1. due to hurt of own self, 2. Due to loss of belongings and 3. Due to loss of human relationships

[359] तरुणी *Tharunee*

[360] तापसाराध्या *Thaapasa-aaradhyaa*

[361] तनुमद्ध्या *Thanu-madhyaa*

[362] तमोपहा *Tama-o-apahaa*

Shloka 80.

चितितत्पदलक्ष्यात्र्था चिदेकरसरूपिणी

स्वात्मानन्दलवीभूतब्रह्माद्यानन्दसन्ततिः ॥८०

Chithi-Tath-pada-lakshya-art'thaa Chith-eka-rasa-roopinee
Swa-aathma-ananda-lavee-bhootha-brahma-aadi-ananda-santhathee

80.

[363]She pure knowledge, awareness be,
She personification of all wisdom be,
[364]She means you are that or that you be,
[365]She the inner self which happiness be
- 139 -

She who is wisdom throughout – Glory,
[366]The Great Bliss making others trival truly,
She Ocean of all the wisdom does be,
If the Wisdom of Brahman a wave be.
- 140 -

---

[363] चिति Chithi

[364] तत्पदलक्ष्यात्र्था Tath-pada-lakshya-art'thaa

[365] चिदेकरसरूपिणी Chith-eka-rasa-roopinee

[366] स्वात्मानन्दलवीभूतब्रह्माद्यानन्दसन्तति Swa-aathma-ananda-lavee-bhootha-brahma-
aady-ananda-santhathee

Shloka 81.

परा प्रत्यक् चितीरूपा पश्यन्ती परदेवता
मद्ध्यमा वैखरीरूपा भक्तमानसहंसिका ॥८१

Paraa Prathyak Chithee-roopa Pashyanthee Para-devathaa
Madhyamaa vaikharee-roopa Bhakta-maanasa-hamsikaa

81.

[367]She who is beyond everything – Glory,
[368]She unclear supreme truth, knowledge be,
She makes us seek wisdom inside surely,
[369]She who sees all within herself – Glory.
- 141 -

[370]She who above everythings be – Glory,
She who gives power to all gods – Glory,
[371]She in second phase of sound wave be,
[372]She who is of the form with words – Glory,
- 142 -

[373]She who lives in the heart of the devotee
As lovely swans - *maanasa saras* legendary,
She who like a swan mythical does be,
Within the lake called the mind – Glory.
- 143 -

---

[367] परा *Paraa*

[368] प्रत्यक् चितीरूपा *Prathyak Chithee-roopa*

[369] पश्यन्ती *Pashyanthee*

[370] परदेवता *Para-devathaa*

[371] मद्ध्यमा *Madhyamaa*

[372] वैखरीरूपा *Vaikharee-roopa*

[373] भक्तमानसहंसिका *Bhakta-maanasa-hamsikaa*

Shloka 82.

कामेश्वरप्राणनाड़ी कृतज्ञा कामपूजिता
श्रृङ्गाररससंपूर्णा जया जालन्तरस्थिता ॥८२

Kama-eswara-praana-naadee Kr'tha-jnaa kaama-poojithaa
Sr'ngaara-rasa-sampoornnaa Jayaa Jaala-anthara-st'thithaa

82.

[374]She life for them who surrendered fully,
All their wants, desires – rule them totally,
[375] She sees all actions, knows all – Glory,
[376]She worshipped for wants fulfillment truly.
- 144 -

She worshipped by God of love – Glory,
[377]She fills human heart with bliss – Glory,
She who is romantically lovely – Glory,
[378] She manifests as victory in the devotee.
- 145 -

She personification of victory be – Glory,
Helps overcome hatred, anger, pride truly,
[379]She who is on *Jalandhara peetha* – Glory,
She who is the purest of the pure – Glory.
- 146 -

---

[374] कामेश्वरप्राणनाड़ी *Kama-eswara-praana-naadee*

[375] कृतज्ञा *Kr'tha-jnaa*

[376] कामपूजिता *kaama-poojithaa*

[377] श्रृङ्गाररससंपूर्णा *Sr'ngaara-rasa-sampoorna*

[378] जया *Jayaa*

[379] जालन्तरस्थिता *Jaala-anthara-st'thithaa*

Shloka 83.

ओड्याणपीठनिलया बिन्दुमण्डलवासिनी
रहोयागक्रमाराध्या रहस्तर्पणतर्पिता ॥८३

Ooedyana-peet'ta-nilayaa Bindu-mandala-vaasinee
Raha-o-yaaga-krama-aaradhya Raha-s-tharpana-tharpithaa

83.

[380]She manifests in the heart of devotee ,
[381]She the centre of the Shri chakra be,
[382]She worshipped in heart of devotee,
[383]She pleased by chants knowing fully.
- 147 -

Shloka 84.

सद्यःप्रसादिनी विश्वसाक्षिणी साक्षिवर्जिता
षडंगदेवतायुक्ता षाड्गुण्यपरिपूरिता ॥८४

Sadyah Prasaadinee Vishwa-saakshinee Saakshi-varjithaa
Shad-anga-devathaa-yuktaa Shaad-gunya-pari-poorithaa

84.

[384] She who is pleased immediately – Glory,
[385]She witness of all in the universe – Glory,
[386]She who not witnessed by anyone – Glory,
She does not have witness for self – Glory.
- 148 -

---

[380] ओड्याणपीठनिलया *Ooedyana-peet'ta-nilayaa*

[381] बिन्दुमण्डलवासिनी *Bindu-mandala-vaasinee*

[382] रहोयागक्रमाराध्या *Raha-o-yaaga-krama-aaradhya*

[383] रहस्तर्पणतर्पिता *Raha-s-tharpana-tharpithaa*

[384] सद्यःप्रसादिनी *Sadyah Prasaadinee*

[385] विश्वसाक्षिणी *Vishwa-saakshinee*

[386] साक्षिवर्जिता *Saakshi-varjithaa*

> She who with six parts does be – Glory,
> [387]She the five senses and mind be – Glory,
> She life which illuminates the human body,
> [388]She complete perfection of six qualities*.
> - 149 -

Shloka 85.

नित्यक्लिन्ना निरुपमा निर्वाणसुखदायिनी
नित्याषोडशिकारूपा श्रीकण्ठार्द्धशरीरिणी ॥८५

Nithya-klinnaa Ni-r-upamaa Nirvaana-sukha-daayinee
Nithyaa-shodashikaa-roopaa Sree-kantta-ardha-shareerinee

85.

> [389]She ever full of kindness and mercy,
> [390]She who uncompared to anything be,
> [391]She frees arrows shot by action surely,
> She who gives redemption fully – Glory.
> - 150 -

> She who frees life from bondage – Glory,
> [392]She manifests as moon phases – Glory,
> [393]She who ardha –nareeswar* be - Glory,
> She half body of Lord Shiv be – Glory.
> - 151 -

---

[387] षडंगदेवतायुक्ता *Shad-anga-devathaa-yuktaa*

[388] षाड्गुण्यपरिपूरिता *Shaad-gunya-pari-poorithaa;*
* *glory, righteousness, fame, wealth, knowledge, non-attachment*

[389] नित्यक्लिन्ना *Nithya-klinnaa*

[390] निरुपमा *Ni-r-upamaa*

[391] निर्वाणसुखदायिनी *Nirvaana-sukha-daayinee*

[392] नित्याषोडशिकारूपा *Nithyaa-shodashikaa-roopaa*

[393] श्रीकण्ठार्द्धशरीरिणी *Sree-kantta-ardha-shareerinee;* * *half female and half male*

Shloka 86.

प्रभावती प्रभारूपा प्रसिद्धा परमेश्वरी

मूलप्रकृतिरव्यक्ता व्यक्ताव्यक्तस्वरूपिणी ॥८६

Prabhaavathee Prabhaa-roopaa Prasidhaa Param-eswaree
Moola-prakr'thi-r-avyakthaa Vyaktaa-avykta-swaroopinee

86.

[394]She lustrous of supernatural powers be,
[395]She illumination of life in the living be,
She rays of sun, moon and fire does be
She who personification of the light be.
- 152 -

[396]She the Self of everybody be – Glory,
She who is famous certainly – Glory,
[397]The great lord who protects all be,
She the ultimate goddess be – Glory.
- 153 -

[398]She the root of entire universe be,
[399]She who unclear and unknowable be,
She who is not clearly seen – Glory,
[400] She visible, not visible in universe be.
- 154 -

---

[394] प्रभावती *Prabhaavathee*

[395] प्रभारूपा *Prabhaa-roopaa*

[396] प्रसिद्धा *Prasiddhaa*

[397] परमेश्वरी *Param-eswaree*

[398] मूलप्रकृति: *Moola-prakrtih*

[399] अव्यक्ता *avyakthaa*

[400] व्यक्ताव्यक्तस्वरूपिणी *Vyaktaa-avykta-swaroopinee*

श्री ललिता सहस्रनाम

5th Shathaka

Shloka 87.

व्यापिनी विविधाकारा विद्याविद्यास्वरूपिणी
महाकमेशनयनकुमुदाह्लादकौमुदी ॥८७॥

Vyaapinee Vividha-aakaara Vidya-avidya-swaroopinee
Maha-kaama-esa-nayana-kumuda-aahlaada-koumudee

87.

[401] She who is spread everywhere – Glory,
[402] She has several different forms – Glory,
[403] She knowledge and ignorance be – Glory,
[404]She full moon, opens Lord's* eyes – Glory.
- 155 -

Shloka 88.

भक्तहार्द्तमोभेदभानुमद्भानुसन्ततिः
शिवदूती शिवाराध्या शिवमूर्तिः शिवंकरी ॥८८॥

Bhakta-haard'da Thama-o-bhaeda Bhaanu-math-bhaanu-santhathih
Shiva-doothee Shiva-aaraadhyaa Shiva-moorthih Shivam-karee

88.

[405]She sun's rays, ends ignorance of devotee,
[406]She who carries the glories to the devotee,
[407]She worshipped by those with great glories,
She worshipped by knowledgeable ones be.
- 156 -

---

[401] व्यापिनी Vyaapinee

[402] विविधाकारा Vividha-aakaara

[403] विद्याविद्यास्वरूपिणी Vidya-avidya-swaroopinee

[404] महाकमेशनयनकुमुदाह्लादकौमुदी Maha-kaama-esa-nayana-kumuda-aahlaada-
koumudee;
* Kameshwara

[405] भक्तहार्द्तमोभेदभानुमद्भानुसन्ततिं Bhakta-haard'da thama-o-bhaeda Bhaanu-math-
bhaanu-santhathih

[406] शिवदूती Shiva-doothee

[407] शिवाराध्या Shiva-aaraadhyaa

[408]She the manifest form of all glories does be,
She the form of Lord Shiv does be – Glory,
[409]She who gives of all glories to devotees
She who makes good to happen – Glory.
- 157 -

Shloka 89.

शिवप्रिया शिवपरा शिष्टेष्टा शिष्टपूजिता

अप्रमेया स्वप्रकाशा मनोवाचामगोचरा ॥८९

Shiva-priyaa Shiva-paraa Shishta-eshtaa Shishta-poojithaa
Apramaeyaa Swa-prakaashaa Mana-o-vaachaam-agoecharaa

89.

[410]She to whom the devotee very dear be,
[411]She who beyond all the glories does be,
[412]She extremely dear to the saintly ones be,
[413]She worshipped by the saintly ones truly.
- 158 -

[414]She who cannot be measured – Glory,
[415]She who is pure illumination – Glory,
[416]She cannot be reached by mind – Glory,
She not understood by words – Glory.
- 159 -

---

[408] शिवमूर्तिः *Shiva-moorthih*

[409] शिवंकरी *Shivam-karee*

[410] शिवप्रिया *Shiva-priyaa*

[411] शिवपरा *Shiva-paraa*

[412] शिष्टेष्टा *Shishta-eshtaa*

[413] शिष्टपूजिता *Shishta-poojithaa*

[414] अप्रमेया *Apramaeyaa*

[415] स्वप्रकाशा *Swa-prakaashaa*

[416] मनोवाचामगोचरा *Mana-o-vaachaam-agoecharaa*

Shloka 90.

चिच्छक्तिश्चेतनारूपा जड़शक्तिर्जडात्मिका
गायत्री व्याहृति: सन्ध्या द्विजवृन्दनिषेविता ॥९०

Chith-Shakti Chethana-roopa Jada-shakti-r-jada-aathmikaa
Gaayathree Vyaahrthi: sandhyaa Dwija-vr'nda-nishevithaa

90.

[417]She strength of holy knowledge – Glory,
[418]She who manifests as life's every activity,
She the power behind all action be – Glory,
[419]She the power to create universe – Glory.
- 160 -

[420]She who manifests as universe – Glory,
[421]She protects those who sings Her glory,
She who is Mother Gayatri clearly – Glory,
[422]She the mantras that chanted be – Glory.
- 161 -

She the grammar from letters be – Glory,
[423]She who joins the day to night – Glory,
She union of souls and God be – Glory,
[424]She the rest after life's activities – Glory.
- 162 -

---

[417] चिच्छक्ति *Chith-shakthi*

[418] चेतनारूपा *Chethana-roopa*

[419] जड़शक्ति *Jada-shaktih*

[420] जडात्मिका *Jada-aathmikaa*

[421] गायत्री *Gaayathree*

[422] व्याहृति: *Vyaahrthih*

[423] सन्ध्या *Sandhyaa*

[424] द्विजवृन्दनिषेविता *Dwija-vr'nda-nishevithaa*

Shloka 91.

तत्वासना तत्वमयी पञ्चकोशान्तरस्थिता
निस्सीममहिमा नित्ययौवना मदशालिनी ॥९१॥

*Thatwa-aasana That-twam-ayee Pancha-koesha-anthara-st'thithaa
Niseema-mahimaa Nithya-youvanaa Mada-shaalinee*

91.

[425]Her very existence the supreme truth be,
The unchanging truth lasting for eternity,
[426]She who you are and that [427]you do be,
[428]She truely addressed, when one called be.
- 163 -

[429]She is the centre of Shri Chakra – Glory,
[430]She with unlimited greatness does be,
[431]She who eternally youthful be - Glory,
[432]She is ecstacy in Her devotee – Glory.
- 164 -

---

[425] तत्वासना *Tathwa-aasana*

[426] तत् *Tath*

[427] त्वं *Twam*

[428] अयी *Ayee*

[429] पञ्चकोशान्तरस्थिता *Pancha-koesha-anthara-st'thithaa*

[430] निस्सीममहिमा *Niseema-mahimaa*

[431] नित्ययौवना *Nithya-youvanaa*

[432] मदशालिनी *Mada-shaalinee*

Shloka 92.

मदघूर्णितरक्ताक्षी मदपाटलगण्डभूः
चन्दनद्रवदिग्धांगी चांबेयकुसुमप्रिया ॥९२॥

*Mada-ghoornnitha-raktha-aakshee Mada-paatala-gandhabhooh
Chandana-drava-digdha-angee Chaambaeya-kusuma-priya*

92.

[433]She causes red eyes due to ecstacy,
[434]And cheeks to become pink – Glory,
[435]Cools as sandal paste life's difficulties,
[436]She adores who sense desire free be.
- 165 -

Shloka 93.

कुशला कोमलाकारा कुरुकुल्ला कुलेश्वरी
कुलकुण्डालया कौलमार्गतत्परसेविता ॥९३॥

*Kushalaa Koemala-aakaara Kurukullaa Kula-eswaree
Kula-kunda-aalaya Koula-maarga-thatpara-saevithaa*

93.

[437]She an expert and intelligent be – Glory,
[438] She who has soft beautiful form – Glory,
[439]She *"kurukulla"* - nectar amid *ida, pingala* be,
[440]She Lord of kundalini in humans does be.
- 166 -

---

[433] मदघूर्णितरक्ताक्षी Mada-ghoornitha-raktha-aakshee

[434] मदपाटलगण्डभूः Mada-paatala-gandhabhooh

[435] चन्दनद्रवदिग्धांगी Chandana-drava-digdha-angee

[436] चांबेयकुसुमप्रिया Chaambaeya-kusuma-priya; *a type of flower from which a bee cannot gather honey*

[437] कुशला Kushalaa

[438] कोमलाकारा Koemala-aakaara

[439] कुरुकुल्ला Kurukullaa

[440] कुलेश्वरी Kula-eswaree

She is the goddess for the clan – Glory,
[441]She whom the kula-kunda the home be,
She light of life unknown to the ordinary,
[442]She pure supreme truth, knowledge be.
- 167 -

Shloka 94.

कुमारगणनाथांबा तुष्ठी: पुष्टिर्मतिर्धृति:
शान्ति: स्वस्थिमती कान्ति: नन्दिनी विघ्ननाशिनी ॥९४॥

Ku-maara-gana-naat'tha-ambaa Thushtih Pushti-r-mathi-r-dhr'thihi
Shaanthih Su-ast'thi-mathee Kaanthi-r-nandinee Vighna-naasinee

94.

[443]She mother of Ganesh and Subrahmany be,
[444]She who ever in complete satisfaction be,
[445]She personification of growth, health be,
- 168 -

[446]She eternally manifests as wisdom – Glory,
[447] She personification of courage be – Glory,
[448]She the peace in hearts of Her devotee be,
[449]She whose existence itself is purity – Glory.
- 169 -

---

[441] कुलकुण्डालया Kula-kunda-aalaya

[442] कौलमार्गतत्परसेविता Koula-maarga-thalpara-saevithaa

[443] कुमारगणनाथांबा Ku-maara-gana-naat'tha-ambaa

[444] तुष्ठी: Thushtih

[445] पुष्टि: Pushtih

[446] मति: Mathih

[447] धृति: Dhr'thih

[448] शान्ति: Shaanthih

[449] स्वस्थिमती Su-ast'thi-mathee

She who keeps well and healthy – Glory,
[450] She personification of light be – Glory,
[451] She who grants great happiness – Glory,
[452] She who removes all obstacles – Glory.,
- 170 -

Shloka 95.

तेजोवती त्रिनयना लोलाक्षी कामरूपिणी

मालिनी हंसिनी माता मलयाचलवासिनी ॥९५

*Theja-o-vathee Thri-nayanaa Loela-akshee Kaama-roopinee
Maalinee Hamsinee Maathaa Malaya-achala-vaasinee*

95.

[453] She source and illumination be – Glory,
[454] She through three paths guides devotee,
Of hearing, thinking, experiencing divinity,
[455] She has desire in Her wandering eyes truly.
- 171 -

[456] She worshiped with garlands adorning be,
[457] She selective as a swan does be – Glory,
Discerns milk from water, good from evil truly,
In Her is the final refuge for the saintly – Glory.
- 172 -

---

[450] *कान्तिः Kaanthih*

[451] *नन्दिनी Nandinee*

[452] *विघ्ननाशिनी Vighna-naasinee*

[453] *तेजोवती Theja-o-vathee*

[454] *त्रिनयना Thri-nayanaa*

[455] *लोलाक्षीकामरूपिणी Loela-akshee kaama-roopinee*

[456] *मालिनी Maalinee*

[457] *हंसिनी Hamsinee*

[458]She mother of the whole universe – Glory,
To Her the devotee go when trouble – Glory,
[459]She stays in the heart of devotee – Glory,
As Malaya mountain* fills with bliss, purity.
- 173 -

Shloka 96.

सुमुखी नलिनी सुभ्रू: शोभना सुरनायिका
कालकण्ठी कान्तिमती क्षोभिणी सूक्ष्मरूपिणी ॥९६॥

Su-mukhee Nalinee Su-bhrooh Shoebhanaa Sura-naayikaa
Kaala-kant'tee Kaanthi-mathee Kshobinee Sookshma-roopinee

96.

[460]She with the most beautiful face – Glory,
She has a pleasing disposition – Glory,
[461]She untouched by world as lotus – Glory,
She who is but tender certainly – Glory.
- 174 -

[462]She with special eyes brows – Glory,
She who has beautiful eyelids – Glory,
[463]She who is always illuminant – Glory,
She who illuminates everything – Glory.
- 175 -

She the illumination of life be – Glory,
She who brings good things – Glory,
[464]She who guides the illuminant – Glory,
She who is the leader of devas – Glory.
- 176 -

---

[458] माता Maathaa

[459] मलयाचलवासिनी Malaya-achala-vaasinee; * a mountain full of sandal trees

[460] सुमुखी Su-mukhee

[461] नलिनी Nalinee

[462] सुभ्रू: Su-bhrooh

[463] शोभना Shoebhanaa

[464] सुरनायिका Sura-naayikaa

[465]She sweetness of voice be – Glory,
The consort of God of death – Glory,
[466]She with great illuminance – Glory,
She who has ethereal luster – Glory.
- 177 -

[467]She desired to create universe – Glory,
Desire to do something with live – Glory,
[468]She too fine to be seen by eye – Glory,
She who has a micro stature – Glory.
- 178 -

Shloka 97.

वज्रेश्वरी वामदेवी वयोवस्थविवर्जिता
सिद्धेश्वरी सिद्धविद्या सीद्धमाता यशस्विनी ॥९७

Vajra-eswaree Vaama-devi Vaya-o-avast'tha-vivarjjithaa
Sidha-eswaree Sidha-vidyaa Sidha-maathaa Yashaswinee

97.

[469]She beauty and power of diamond be,
She unchange with age does be – Glory,
[470]The lord of all beauty and saintly – Glory,
[471]She unaffected by effects of time – Glory.
- 179 -

---

[465] *कालकण्ठी Kaala-kant'tee*
[466] *कान्तिमती Kaanthi-mathee*
[467] *क्षोभिणी Kshobinee*
[468] *सूक्ष्मरूपिणी Sookshma-roopinee*
[469] *वज्रेश्वरी Vajra-eswaree*
[470] *वामदेवी Vaama-devi*
[471] *वयोवस्थविवर्जिता Vaya-o-avast'tha-vivarjithaa*

---

[472]The lord of all acheivements be – Glory,
[473]She manifests as acheivements – Glory.
[474]She mother of all acheivements – Glory,
[475]She with great fame and name – Glory,

- 180 -

Shloka 98.

विशुद्धिचक्रनिलयाऽऽरक्तवर्णा त्रिलोचना

खट्वाङ्गादिप्रहरणा वदनैकसमन्विता ॥९८

*Vishudhi-charka-nilayaa Aa-raktha-varnnaa Thri-loechanaa
Khadvanga-aadi-praharana Vadana-eka-sama-anwithaa*

98.

[476]She is in sixteen petalled lotus – Glory,
[477]She who with a mild red colour – Glory,
[478]She who with the three eyes – Glory,
Sees past, present and future – all Glory.

- 181 -

[479]She holds a club with human head – Glory,
She who has arms like the sword – Glory,
She who attacks the evil ones – Glory,
[480]She who with a single face be – Glory.

- 182 -

---

[472] सिद्धेश्वरी *Sidha-eswaree*

[473] सिद्धविद्या *Sidha-vidyaa*

[474] सीद्धमाता *Sidha-maathaa*

[475] यशस्विनी *Yashaswinee*

[476] विशुद्धिचक्रनिलया *Vishudhi-charka-nilayaa*

[477] आरक्तवर्णा *Aa-raktha-varnaa*

[478] त्रिलोचना *Thri-loechanaa*

[479] खट्वाङ्गादिप्रहरणा *Khadvanga-aadi-praharana*

[480] वदनैकसमन्विता *Vadana-i-eka-sama-anwithaa*

Shloka 99.

पायसान्नप्रिया त्वकस्था पशुलोकभयंकरी
अमृतातिमहाशक्तिसंवृता डाकिनीश्वरी ॥९९॥

Payasa-anna-priyaa Twak-st'tha Pashu-loeka-bhayam-karee
Amr'tha-aadi-maha-Shakti-samvr'thaa Daakini-eeswaree

99.

[481]She worshiped with rice and milk – Glory,
She likes sweet rice as *Payasam* – Glory,
[482]She manifests as skin sensation – Glory,
She lives in sensibility of the skin – Glory.
- 183 -

[483]She creates fear in the evil heart – Glory,
Binds by ropes of their actions – Glory,
[484]She centre of great power, deathless be,
[485]She also known as 'dakineeswari' – Glory.
- 184 -

---

[481] पायसान्नप्रिया *Paayasa-anna-priyaa*

[482] त्वकस्था *Twak-st'tha*

[483] पशुलोकभयंकरी *Pashu-loeka-bhayam-karee*

[484] अमृतातिमहाशक्तिसंवृता *Amr'tha-aadi-maha-shakthi-samvr'thaa*

[485] डाकिनीश्वरी *Daakini-eeswaree*

Shloka 100.

अनाहताब्जनिलया श्यामाभा वदनद्वया
दंष्ट्रोज्ज्वलाऽक्षमालादिधरा रुधिरसंस्थिता ॥१००

Anaahatha-abja-nilayaa Shayaama-bhaa Vadana-dwayaa
Damshtra-o-ujwalaa Aksha-maala-aadi-dharaa Rudhira-sam-st'thithaa
                                                                          100.

[486]She lives in the petalled lotus – Glory,
[487]She black and beautiful in meditation be,
[488]She who with two faces does be – Glory,
[489]She with feared fangs attacks evil – Glory.
                    - 185 -

[490]She wears a garland of weapons – Glory,
She who attacks the evil ones – Glory,
[491]She who but exists in blood – Glory,
Gives it the life supporting properties.
                    - 186 -

---

[486] अनाहताब्जनिलया Anaahatha-ap-ja-nilayaa

[487] श्यामाभा Shayaama-bhaa

[488] वदनद्वया Vadana-dwayaa

[489] दंष्ट्रोज्ज्वला Damshtra-o-ujwalaa

[490] अक्षमालादिधरा Aksha-maala-aadi-dharaa

[491] रुधिरसंस्थिता Rudhira-sam-st'thithaa

Shloka 101.

कालरात्र्यादिशक्त्यौघवृता स्निग्धौदनप्रिया

महावीरेन्द्रवरदा राकिण्यंबास्वरूपिणी ॥१०१

Kaala-raathri-aadi-shakti-aougha-vr'thaa Snigdha-oedana-priyaa
Maha-veera-e-indra-vara-daa Raakiny-ambaa-swa-roopinee

101.

[492]She centre of great destructive powers be,
Fills the evil doers with great fear – Glory,
[493]She revered with offerings of rice with ghee,
She who likes Ghee mixed rice – Glory,
- 187 -
[494]She blesses heros and sages – Glory,
Who beyond alertness, dream, sleep be,
She who gives blessings to such – Glory,
[495] She who has names like *rakini* – Glory.
- 188 -

Shloka 102.

मणिपूरब्जनिल्या वदनत्रयसंयुता

वज्रादिकायुधोपेता डामर्य्यादिभिरावृता॥१०२

Mani-poora-abja-nilayaa Vadana-thraya-samyuthaa
Vajra-aadikaa-aayudha-o-upaedaa Daamari-aadibhi-r-aavr'thaa

102.

[496]She lives in ten petalled lotus – Glory,
[497]She who with three faces be – Glory,
[498]She has weapons of diamonds – Glory,
[499]Surrounded by Goddess like Damari.
- 189 -

---

[492] कालरात्र्यादिशक्त्यौघवृता Kaala-raathri-aadi-shakti-aougha-vr'thaa

[493] स्निग्धौदनप्रिया Snigdha-oedana-priyaa

[494] महावीरेन्द्रवरदा Maha-veera-e-indra-vara-daa

[495] राकिण्यंबास्वरूपिणी Raakiny-ambaa-swa-roopinee

[496] मणिपूरब्जनिल्या Mani-poora-abja-nilayaa

[497] वदनत्रयसंयुता Vadana-thraya-samyuthaa

[498] वज्रादिकायुधोपेता Vajra-aadikaa-aayudha-upaedaa

[499] डामर्य्यादिभिरावृता Daamari-aadibhi-r-aavr'thaa

Shloka 103.

रक्तवर्णा मांसनिष्ठा गुडान्नप्रीतमानसा
समस्तभक्तसुखदा लाकिन्यंबास्वरूपिणी ॥१०३

Raktha-varnnaa Maamsa-nisht'taa Guda-anna-preetha-maanasaa
Samastha-bhakta-sukha-daa Laakini-amba-swa-roopinee

103.

[500] She is of the colour of blood – Glory,
[501] She the power of the muscles – Glory,
[502] She who likes rice with jiggery – Glory,
She the sweetness of all life be – Glory.

- 190 -

[503] She grants of joy, well being to devotee,
She gives pleasure to deserving – Glory,
[504] She is famous as *"Lakini"* truly – Glory,
Who described by many names – Glory.

- 191 -

---

[500] रक्तवर्णा *Raktha-varnaa*

[501] मांसनिष्ठा *Maamsa-nisht'taa*

[502] गुडान्नप्रीतमानसा *Guda-anna-preetha-maanasaa*

[503] समस्तभक्तसुखदा *Samastha-bhakta-sukha-daa*

[504] लाकिन्यंबास्वरूपिणी *Laakini-amba-swa-roopinee*

6th Shathaka

Shloka 104.

स्वाधिष्ठानांबुजगता चतुर्व्वक्त्रमनोहरा
शूलाद्यायुधसम्पन्ना पीतवर्णाऽतिगर्व्विता॥१०४

*Swa-adhishtaana-ambu-ja-gathaa Chatu-r-vaktra-mana-o-haraa
Shoola-aadi-aayudha-sampannaa Peetha-varnaa-athi-garvvithaa*

104.

[505]She in *'Swaadishtan chakra'* above spine tip be,
[506]She who is beautiful with four faces – Glory,
[507]She holds a trident, other weapons – Glory,
She who attacks evil unrelentingly – Glory.
- 192 -

[508]She loved with a yellow colour – Glory,
She who is of a golden colour – Glory,
[509]She not reachable to humans ordinary,
She who is exceptionally proud – Glory.
- 193 -

---

[505] स्वाधिष्ठानांबुजगता *Swa-adhishtan-ambu-ja-gathaa*

[506] चतुर्व्वक्त्रमनोहरा *Chatu-r-vaktra-mana-o-haraa*

[507] शूलाद्यायुधसम्पन्ना *Shoola-aadi-aayudha-sampannaa*

[508] पीतवर्णा *Peetha-varnnaa*

[509] अतिगर्व्विता *Athi-garvvithaa*

Shloka 105.

मेदोनिष्ठा मधुप्रीता बन्धिन्यादिसमन्विता
दध्यन्नासक्तहृदया काकिनीरूपधारिणी ॥१०५

Meda-o-nishtaa Madhu-preethaa Bandhini-aadi-sama-anwithaa
Dadhy-anna-aasaktha-hr'dayaa Kaakinee-roopa-dhaarinee

105.

[510]She gives power to fatty tissues body,
She who is in the fatty layer – Glory,
[511]She worshiped with offerings of honey,
[512]She centre of Bandini and other powers be.
- 194 -
She is surrounded by Shaktis – Glory,
[513]She worshipped by rice and curd – Glory.
[514]She is famous as 'Kaakinee ' truly – Glory,
Who described by many names – Glory.
- 195 -

Shloka 106.

मूलाधारांबुजारूढ़ा पञ्चवक्त्रास्थिसंस्थिता
अङ्कुशादिप्रहरणा वरदादिनिषेविता ॥१०६

Moola-aadhaara-ambu-ja-aaroodhaa Pancha-vakthraa Ast'thi-samst'thithaa
Ankusha-aadi-praharanaa Varadaa-aadi-nishevithaa

106.

[515]She sits on mooladhar kamal* – Glory,
Which basic support of humans be – Glory,
[516]She who is having five faces – Glory,
[517]She gives power to the bones – Glory.
- 196 -

---

[510] मेदोनिष्ठा Meda-o-nishtaa

[511] मधुप्रीता Madhu-preethaa

[512] बन्धिन्यादिसमन्विता Bandhini-aadi-sama-anwithaa

[513] दध्यन्नासक्तहृदया Dadhy-anna-aasaktha-hr'dayaa

[514] काकिनीरूपधारिणी Kaakinee-roopa-dhaarinee

[515] मूलाधारांबुजारूढ़ा Moola-aadhaara-ambu-ja-aaroodhaa; *lotus

[516] पञ्चवक्त्रा Pancha-vakthraa

[517] अस्थिसंस्थिता Ast'thi-samst'thithaa

She who resides in the bones – Glory,
[518]She has a stick, other weapons – Glory,
[519]She is attended by 'varadaa' – Glory,
Surrounded by other shaktis – Glory
- 197 -

Shloka 107.

मुद्गौदनासक्तचित्ता साकीन्यंबास्वरूपिणी
आज्ञाचक्राब्जनिलया शुक्लवर्णा षडानना ॥१०७

Mudga-oudana-aasaktha-chit'thaa Saakini-ambaa-swa-roopinee
Aajna-chakra-abja- nilayaa Shukla-varnnaa Shad-aananaa

107.

[520]She likes rice and green grams – Glory,
[521]She who is known as 'Saakini' – Glory,
Who described by many names – Glory,
[522] She sits on *Agna chakra* a lotus – Glory.
- 198 -

She sits on the wheel of order – Glory,
[523]She whom devotee in mediation truly,
Appreciate as a white colour – Glory,
[524]She who with six faces – Glory.
- 199 -

---

[518] अङ्कुशादिप्रहरणा Ankusha-aadi-praharanaa

[519] वरदादिनिषेविता Varadaa-aadi-nishevithaa

[520] मुद्गौदनासक्तचित्ता Mudga-odana-aasaktha-chit'thaa

[521] साकीन्यंबास्वरूपिणी Saakini-ambaa-swa-roopinee

[522] आज्ञाचक्राब्जनिलया Aajna-chakra-abja-nilayaa

[523] शुक्लवर्णा Shukla-varnna

[524] षडानना Shad-aananaa

Shloka 108.

मज्जासंस्था हंसवती मुख्यशक्तिसमन्विता
हरिद्रान्नैकरसिका हाकिनीरूपधारिणी ॥१०८

Majjaa-samst'thaa Hamsa-vathee mukhya-shakti-sama-anwithaa
Haridra-anna-i-eka-rasikaa Haakinee-roopa-dhaarinee

108.

[525]She marrow power to yield blood – Glory,
[526]She the power *'Hamsa-vathee'* be – Glory,
[527]She revered with rice and turmeric – Glory,
[528]She who is known as ' Haakinee ' – Glory.
- 200 -

Shloka 109.

सहस्रदलपद्मस्था सर्व्ववर्णोपशोभिता
सर्वायुधधरा शुक्लसंस्थिता सर्वतोमुखी ॥१०९

Sahasra-dala-padma-st'thaa Sarva-varnna-o-upa-shobhithaa
Sarva-aayudha-dharaa Shukla-sam-st'thithaa Sarvatha-o-mukhee

109.

[529] She sits on thousand petalled lotus – Glory,
[530] She who shines in all colours – Glory,
[531]She clutches many weapons – Glory,
She who attacks the evil ones – Glory.
- 201 -

---

[525] मज्जासंस्था Majjaa-samst'thaa
[526] हंसवती मुख्यशक्तिसमन्विता Hamsa-vathee mukhya-shakti-sama-anwithaa
[527] हरिद्रान्नैकरसिका Haridra-anna-i-eka-rasikaa
[528] हाकिनीरूपधारिणी Haakinee-roopa-dhaarinee
[529] सहस्रदलपद्मस्था Sahasra-dala-padma-st'thaa
[530] सर्व्ववर्णोपशोभिता Sarva-varnna-o-upa-shobhithaa
[531] सर्वायुधधरा Sarva-aayudha-dharaa

[532]She the power of reproduction – Glory,
She who is in *shukla* or semen – Glory,
[533]She who has faces all over – Glory,
She sees all things everywhere – Glory.
- 202 -

Shloka 110.

सर्वौदनप्रीतचित्ता याकिन्यंबास्वरूपिणी
स्वाहा स्वधाऽमतिर्मेधा श्रुति: स्मृतिरनुत्तमा ॥११०

Sarva-oedana-preetha-chit'thaa Yaakini-amba-swa-roopinee
Swaahaa Swadhaa Amathi-r-maedhaa-shruthih Smr'thi-r-anu-ut'thamaa
110.

[534]She worshiped with any offering – Glory,
[535]She who is known as 'Yaakini ' – Glory,
[536]She who says what is good– Glory,
[537]She addressed when praying for the dead
- 203 -

[538]She manifests as material wealth – Glory,
To he who without intelligence be – Glory,
She who is ignorance clearly – Glory,
[539]She who is intelligence – Glory,
- 204 -

---

[532] शुक्लसंस्थिता *Shukla-sam-st'thithaa*

[533] सर्वतोमुखी *Sarvatha-o-mukhee*

[534] सर्वौदनप्रीतचित्ता *Sarva-oedana-preetha-chit'thaa*

[535] याकिन्यंबास्वरूपिणी *Yaakini-amba-swa-roopinee*

[536] स्वाहा *Swaahaa*

[537] स्वधा *Swadhaa*

[538] अमति: मेधा *Amathi Maedhaa*

[539] मेधा *Maedhaa*

540She who is core of vedas – Glory,
541She who is forgetfulness – Glory,
She who helps forget sorrow – Glory,
542She who has none greater – Glory,
- 205 -

Shloka 111.

पुण्यकीर्तिः पुण्यलभ्या पुण्यश्रवणकीर्त्तना
पुलोमजार्च्चिता बन्धमोचिनी बर्बरालका ॥१११॥

*Puniya-keerthih Puniya-labhyaa Puniya-shravana-keertthanaa
Pulomaja-aarchitha Bandha-moechinee Barbara-alakaa*

111.

543She whose praise purifies totally – Glory,
She is famous for good deeds – Glory,
544She experienced only by saintly – Glory,
She is attained by good deeds – Glory.
- 206 -

545She purifies who sing or hear of Her – Glory,
546She is worshipped by *'Pulomaja'* – Glory,
Who is the consort of Lord Indra – Glory,
547She frees bondage by ignorance – Glory,
548Her hair is beautiful and curly – Glory.
- 207 -

---

540 श्रुतिः *Shruthih*

541 स्मृतिः *Smr'thi*

542 अनुत्तमा *An-ut'thamaa*

543 पुण्यकीर्तिः *Puniya-keerthih*

544 पुण्यलभ्या *Puniya-labhyaa*

545 पुण्यश्रवणकीर्त्तना *Puniya-shravana-keerthanaa*

546 पुलोमजार्च्चिता *Pulomaja-architha*

547 बन्धमोचिनी *Bandha-moechinee*

548 बर्बरालका *Barbara-alakaa*

Shloka 112.

विमर्शरूपिणी विद्या वियदादिजगत्प्रसू:
सर्वव्याधिप्रशमनी सर्वमृत्युनिवारिणी ॥११२

Vimarsha-roopinee Vidyaa Viyath-aadi-jagath-prasooh
Sarva-vyaadhi-prashamanee Sarva-mr'thyu-nivaaranee

112.

[549]She manifests as words, forms – Glory,
She who is hidden from view – Glory,
[550]She manifests as knowledge – Glory,
She who is the "learning" – Glory.
- 208 -

[551]She created earth and sky – Glory,
[552]She who cures all diseases – Glory,
[553]She saves devotee from death – Glory,
Frees from cycle of birth, death – Glory.
- 209 -

---

[549] *विमर्शरूपिणी Vimarsha-roopinee*

[550] *विद्या Vidyaa*

[551] *वियदादिजगत्प्रसू Viyath-aadi-jagath-prasooh*

[552] *सर्वव्याधिप्रशमनी Sarva-vyaadhi-prashamanee*

[553] *सर्वमृत्युनिवारिणी Sarva-mr'thyu-nivaaranee*

Shloka 113.

अग्रगण्याऽचिन्त्यरूपा कलिकल्मषनाशिनी
कात्यायनी कालहन्त्री कमलाक्षनिषेविता ॥११३

Agra-ganyaa Achinthya-roopaa Kali-kalmasha-naashinee
Kaathiyayanee Kaala-hanthree Kamala-aksha-nishevithaa

113.

[554]She first before anything else – Glory,
[555] She who is beyond thought – Glory,
[556] She removes ills in dark age – Glory,
[557]She enlightens entire universe – Glory.
- 210 -

[558]She destroys effects of time – Glory,
She who is beyond all time – Glory,
She who kills god of death – Glory,
[559] She adored by lotus eyed Vishnu – Glory.
- 211 -

---

[554] अग्रगण्या Agra-ganyaa

[555] अचिन्त्यरूपा Achinthya-roopaa

[556] कलिकल्मषनाशिनी Kali-kalmasha-naashinee

[557] कात्यायनी Kaathiyayanee

[558] कालहन्त्री Kaala-hanthree

[559] कमलाक्षनिषेविता Kamala-aksha-nishevithaa

Shloka 114.

तांबूलपूरितमुखी दाडिमीकुसुमप्रभा
मृगाक्षी मोहिनी मुख्या मृडानी मित्ररूपिणी ॥११४

Thaamboola-pooritha-mukhee Dadimee-kusuma-prabhaa
Mr'ga-akshee Moehinee Mukhyaa Mr'daanee Mithra-roopinee
114.

[560] Her mouth filled with Thambool* – Glory,
[561] She beauty of 'dadimee' flower be – Glory,
[562] She with eyes as beautiful as deer – Glory,
[563] She charms universe with deeds – Glory.
- 212 -

[564] She who was the very first to exist – Glory,
[565] She who gives all the pleasures – Glory,
[566] She who in the form of a friend be – Glory,
She who is of the form of the Sun – Glory.
- 213 -

---

[560] तांबूलपूरितमुखी *Thaamboola-pooritha-mukhee; * betel leaves, nut and lime*
[561] दाडिमीकुसुमप्रभा *Daadimee-kusuma-prabhaa*
[562] मृगाक्षी *Mr'ga-akshee*
[563] मोहिनी *Moehinee*
[564] मुख्या *Mukhyaa*
[565] मृडानी *Mr'daanee*
[566] मित्ररूपिणी *Mithra-roopinee*

Shloka 115.

नित्यतृप्ता भक्तनिधि: नियन्त्री निखिलेश्वरी

मैत्र्यादिवासनालभ्या महाप्रलयसाक्षिणी ॥११५

Nithya-thr'pthaa Bhaktha-nidhi-r-niyanthree Nikhila-eeswaree
Maithrya-aadi-vaasanaa-labhyaa Maha-pralaya-saakshinee

115.

[567]She who is always satisfied – Glory,
[568]She treasured by devotee – Glory,
She wealth to the devotee – Glory,
[569]She controls the universe – Glory.

- 214 -

[570]She the Lord of universe – Glory,
[571]She reached by friendship – Glory,
[572]She is the sole witness – Glory,
Of the Universe's end – Glory.

- 215 -

---

[567] *नित्यतृप्ता Nithya-thr'pthaa*

[568] *भक्तनिधि: Bhaktha-nidhih*

[569] *नियन्त्री Niyanthree*

[570] *निखिलेश्वरी Nikhila-eeswaree*

[571] *मैत्र्यादिवासनालभ्या Maithry-aadi-vaasanaa-labhyaa*

[572] *महाप्रलयसाक्षिणी Maha-pralaya-saakshinee*

Shloka 116.

पराशक्तिः परानिष्टा प्रज्ञानघनरूपिणी

माद्ध्वीपानालसा मत्ता मातृकावर्णरूपिणी॥११६

Paraa-sakthi Paraa-nisht'taa Prajnaana-Ghana-roopinee
Maadhwee-paana-alasaa Mat'thaa Maathr'kaa-varnna-roopinee
116.

[573]She power beyond all power – Glory,
She who is the end strength – Glory,
[574]She with great firmness be – Glory,
She the ultimate shelter be – Glory.
- 216 -

[575]She pure, supreme knowledge be,
[576]She intoxicated by nectar of bliss be
[577] She who appears to faint – Glory,
[578]She alphabets, colour, shape be – Glory
- 217 -

---

[573] पराशक्तिः *Paraa-shakthi*

[574] परानिष्टा *Paraa-nisht'taa*

[575] प्रज्ञानघनरूपिणी *Prajnaana-Ghana-roopinee*

[576] माद्ध्वीपानालसा *Maadhwee-paana-alasaa*

[577] मत्ता *Mat'thaa*

[578] मातृकावर्णरूपिणी *Maathr'kaa-varnna-roopinee*

Shloka 117.

महाकैलासनिलया मृणालमृदुदोर्ल्लता
महनीया दयामूर्त्ति महासाम्राज्यशालिनी ॥११७

Maha-kailaasa-nilayaa Mr'naala-mrdu-doer-lathaa
Mahaneeyaa Dayaa-moorthih Mahaa-saam-raajya-shaalinee
117.

[579] She who sits on Maha Kailasa – Glory,
[580] Her arms tender as lotus stalk be – Glory,
[581] She worthy of being worshipped – Glory,
[582] She who the manifest form of kindness be.
- 218 -

She the personification of mercy – Glory,
[583] She the ruler of all the worlds – Glory,
She for amusement, rules world – Glory,
She the chef of all the worlds be – Glory.
- 219 -

---

[579] महाकैलासनिलया Maha-kailaasa-nilayaa
[580] मृणालमृदुदोर्ल्लता Mr'naala-mr'du-doer-lathaa
[581] महनीया Mahaneeyaa
[582] दयामूर्त्तिः Dayaa-moorthih
[583] महासाम्राज्यशालिनी Mahaa-saamraajya-shaalinee

Shloka 118.

आत्मविद्या महाविद्या श्रीविद्या कामसेविता

श्रीषोडशाक्षरीविद्या त्रिकूटा कामकोटिका ॥११८

Aathma-vidyaa Maha-vidyaa Sree-vidyaa Kaama-saevithaa
Sree-shodasha-aksharee-vidyaa Thri-kootaa Kaama-koetikaa
118.

[584] She who is the science of soul – Glory,
[585] She who is the great knowledge – Glory,
[586] She knowledge of Goddess be – Glory,
[587] She deified by who desire things worldly.
- 220 -

"She worshipped by God of Love – Glory,
[588] She form of Shri Vidya mantra be – Glory,
[589] She experienced in three forms* - Glory,
[590] She sits on *Kama Koti peetha** – Glory,
- 221 -

---

[584] आत्मविद्या *Aathma-vidyaa*

[585] महाविद्या *Maha-vidyaa*

[586] श्रीविद्या *Sree-vidyaa*

[587] कामसेविता *Kaama-saevithaa*

[588] श्रीषोडशाक्षरीविद्या *Sree-shodasha-aksharee-vidyaa*

[589] त्रिकूटा *Thri-kootaa; * as creator, protector, destroyer or alertness, sleep, dream or saintliness, disturbance, lethargy or as Rig, Yaju, Saama vedas*
[590] कामकोटिका *Kaama-koetikaa; *peak of desire*

Shloka 119.

कटाक्षकिंकरीभूतकमलाकोटिसेविता

शिरस्थिता चन्द्रनिभा फालस्थेन्द्रधनुप्रभा ॥११

Kata-aksha-kim-karee-bhootha-kamala-koeti-saevithaa
Shirah-st'thithaa Chandra-nibhaa Ppaala-st'tha-e-indra-dhanu-prabhaa

119.

[591]Her glance bring millions to devotees,
[592]She who is in the real head – Glory,
[593] She who is like the full moon – Glory,
And Her beauty is unmatched – Glory.
- 222 -

[594]She rises to *'Aajna chakra'* – Glory,
She who is in the forehead – Glory,
[595]She manifests in heart of devotee,
She who is like the rain bow – Glory.
- 223 -

---

[591] कटाक्षकिंकरीभूतकमलाकोटिसेविता *Kata-aksha-kim-karee-bhootha-kamala-koeti-saevithaa*
[592] शिरस्थिता *Shirah st'thithaa*
[593] चन्द्रनिभा *Chandra-nibhaa*
[594] फालस्था *Ppaala-st'thaa*
[595] इन्द्रधनुप्रभा *Indra-dhanu-prabhaa*

Shloka 120.

हृदयस्था रविप्रख्या त्रिकोणान्तरदीपिका
दाक्षायणी दैत्यहन्त्री दक्षयज्ञविनाशिनी ॥१२०॥

Hr'daya-st'thaa Ravi-prakhyaa Thri-koena-anthra-deepikaa
Daakshaayanee Daithya-hanthree Daksha-yajna-vinaashinee
                                                    120.

[596] She who is in the heart – Glory,
[597] She beauty of the sun – Glory,
She has glow of the sun – Glory,
[598] She like a light in a triangle – Glory.
- 224 -

[599] She Aswini, other constellations be,
She legendary daughter of Daksha be,
[600] She destroys evil thoughts – Glory,
[601] She destroys Rudra's sacrifice – Glory,
- 225 -

---

[596] हृदयस्था Hr'daya-st'thaa

[597] रविप्रख्या Ravi-prakhyaa

[598] त्रिकोणान्तरदीपिका Thri-koena-anthra-deepikaa

[599] दाक्षायणी Daakshaayanee

[600] दैत्यहंत्री Daithya-hanthree

[601] दक्षयज्ञविनाशिनी Daksha-yajna-vinaashinee

7th Shathaka

Shloka 121.

दरान्दोलितदीर्घाक्षी दरहासोज्ज्वलन्मुखी
गुरुमूर्त्तिर्गुणनिधिः गोमाता गुहजन्मभूः ॥१२१॥

Dara-aandoelitha-deergha-akshi Dara-haasa-o-ujwalan-mulkhee
Gurumoorthi-r-guna-nidhi-r-goe-maathaa Guha-janma-bhooh
                                                          121.

[602]Her eyes remove fear from devotee – Glory,
[603]She happy with saintly, angry with evil be,
[604]She who is the supreme truth – Glory,
She who is the real teacher truly – Glory.
- 226 -

[605]She ultimate source of all goodness be,
She the treasure house of good qualities,
[606]The mother of all these surely – Glory,
[607]She birth place of Lord Subrahmanya be.
- 227 -

---

[602] दरान्दोलितदीर्घाक्षी *Dara-aandoelitha-deergha-akshi*

[603] दरहासोज्ज्वलन्मुखी *Dara-haasa-o-ujjwalan-mukee*

[604] गुरुमूर्त्तिः *Gurumoorthih*

[605] गुणनिधिः *Guna-nidhih*

[606] गोमाता *Goe-maathaa*

[607] गुहजन्मभूः *Guha-janma-bhooh*

Shloka 122.

देवेशी दण्डनीतिस्था दहराकाशरूपिणी

प्रतिपन्मुख्यराकान्ततिथिमण्डलपूजिता ॥१२२

Deva-esi Danda-neethi-st'thaa Dahara-aakaasha-roopinee
Prathipan-mukhya-raakaa-antha-thit'thi-mandala-poojithaa

122.

[608]She who is the goddess of Gods – Glory,
[609]She who judges and punishes – Glory,
[610] She who is of the form of sky – Glory,
[611]She who is worshipped all days – Glory.
- 228 -

Shloka 123.

कलात्मिका कलानाथा काव्यालापविनोदिनी

सचामररमावाणी सव्यदक्षिणसेविता॥१२३

Kala-aathmikaa Kala-naat'thaa Kaavya-aalaapa-vinoedinee
Sa-chaamara-rema-vaanee-savya-dakshina-saevithaa

123.

[612]She who is the soul of arts – Glory,
[613]She who is the chief of arts – Glory,
[614]She worshipped by chants devotedly,
[615]She fanned by Lakshmi* and Saraswathi**.
- 229 -

---

[608] देवेशी *Deva-esi*

[609] दण्डनीतिस्था *Danda-neethi-st'thaa*

[610] दहराकाशरूपिणी *Dahara-aakaasha-roopinee*

[611] प्रतिपन्मुख्यराकान्ततिथिमण्डलपूजिता *Prathipan-mukhya-raakaa-antha-thit'thi-mandala-poojithaa*

[612] कलात्मिका *Kala-aathmikaa*

[613] कलानाथा *Kalaa-naat'thaa*

[614] काव्यालापविनोदिनी *Kaavya-aalaapa-vinoedinee*

[615] सचामररमावाणी सव्यदक्षिणसेविता *Sa-chaamara-rema-vaanee-savya-dakshina-saevithaa*
  * Goddess of Wealth
  * Goddess of Knowledge

Shloka 124.

आदिशक्तिरमेयाऽऽत्मा परमा पावनाकृति:
अनेककोटीब्रह्माण्डजननी दिव्यविग्रहा ॥१२४

Aadi-Shakti-r-amaeya-athma Paramaa Paavana-aakr'thih
Anaeka-koeti-brahma-anda-jananee Divya-vigrahaa

124.

[616] She who is the primeval force – Glory,
[617] She who cannot be measured – Glory,
[618] She who is the Atma – the soul – Glory,
[619] She who is better than all others – Glory.
- 230 -

[620] She personification of purity be – Glory,
[621] She mother to limitless universes be,
[622] She who is divinity manifest – Glory,
She who is beautifully made – Glory.
- 231 -

---

[616] *आदिशक्ति: Aadi-shakthi*

[617] *अमेया Amaeya*

[618] *आत्मा Aathma*

[619] *परमा Paramaa*

[620] *पावनाकृति: Paavana-aakr'thee*

[621] *अनेककोटीब्रह्माण्डजननी Anaeka-koeti-brahma-anda-jananee*

[622] *दिव्यविग्रहा Divya-vigrahaa*

Shloka 125.

क्लींकारी केवला गुह्या कैवल्यपददायिनी
त्रिपुरा त्रिजगद्वन्द्या त्रिमूर्त्तिस्त्रिदशेश्वरी ॥१२५

Kleem-kaaree Kaevalaa Guhyaa Kaivalya-pada-daayinee
Thri-pura Thri-jagath-vandya Thri-moorthy-s-thri-dasa-eswaree
125.

[623]She is shape of "Klim" – Glory,
[624]She who is she herself – Glory,
[625]She who is the secret – Glory,
[626] She redeems, gives status – Glory.
- 232 -

[627]She lives in three aspects* – Glory,
[628] She revered in three worlds* – Glory,
[629]She manifests in three forms* – Glory,
[630]The lord of the three states* – Glory.
- 233 -

---

[623] *क्लींकारी Kleem-kaaree*

[624] *केवला Kaevalaa*

[625] *गुह्या Guhyaa*

[626] *कैवल्यपददायिनी Kaivalya-pada-daayinee*

[627] *त्रिपुरा Thri-pura;* * alertness, dream and sleep state or mind, intelligence, and life

[628] *त्रिजगद्वन्द्या Thri-jagath-vandya;* * saintliness, activity and ignorance

[629] *त्रिमूर्त्तिः Thri-moorthih;* * Creator, Protector and Destroyer

[630] *त्रिदशेश्वरी Thri-dasa-eswaree;* * alertness, dream and sleep or knowledge, glory and wealth

Shloka 126.

त्र्यक्षरी दिव्यगन्धाढ्या सिन्दूरतिलकाञ्चिता
उमा शैलेन्द्रतनया गौरी गन्धर्व्वसेविता ॥१२६

Thri-aksharee Divya-gandha-aadyaa Sindoora-thilaka-anjitha
Uma shaila-e-indra-thanaya Gouree Gandharva-saevithaa

126.

[631] She the form of three letters be – Glory,
[632] She who has divine fragrances – Glory,
[633] She adorns sindhoor on forehead – Glory,
[634] She measures supreme knowledge truly,
- 234 -

She who is in the divine "om" – Glory,
[635] She lead to destination of mind – Glory,
[636] She who with the colour of gold be,
[637] She worshipped by the sun – Glory.
- 235 -

---

[631] त्र्यक्षरी *Thri-aksharee*

[632] दिव्यगन्धाढ्या *Divya-gandha-aadyaa*

[633] सिन्दूरतिलकाञ्चिता *Sindoora-thilaka-anjitha*

[634] उमा *Uma*

[635] शैलेन्द्रतनया *Shaila-e-indratha-naya*

[636] गौरी *Gouree*

[637] गन्धर्व्वसेविता *Gandharva-saevithaa*

Shloka 127.

विश्वगर्भा स्वर्णगर्भाऽवरदा वागधीश्वरी
ध्यानगम्याऽपरिच्छेद्या ज्ञानदा ज्ञानविग्रहा ॥१२७

Vishwa-garbhaa Swarna-garbhaa-avara-daa Vaak-adi-eeswaree
Dhyaana-gamyaa-aparich'chaedyaa Jnaana-daa Jnaana-vigrahaa
127.

[638]She in whom contains the universe surely,
Wwho carries universe in her belly – Glory,
[639] She who is personification of gold – Glory,
[640]She who punishes, destroys evil – Glory.
- 236 -

[641]She who is the lord of all words – Glory,
She is the goddess of the words – Glory,
[642]She got by complete surrender – Glory,
She be attained by meditation – Glory.
- 237 -

[643]She who cannot be measured – Glory,
She who cannot be predicted– Glory,
[644]She gives supreme knowledge – Glory,
[645]She embodiment of knowledge – Glory.
- 238 -

---

[638] विश्वगर्भा *Vishwa-garbhaa*

[639] स्वर्णगर्भा *Swarna-garbhaa*

[640] अवरदा *Avara-daa*

[641] वागधीश्वरी *Vaak-adi-eeswaree*

[642] ध्यानगम्या *Dhyaana-gamyaa*

[643] अपरिच्छेद्या *Aparich'chaedyaa*

[644] ज्ञानदा *Jnaana-daa*

[645] ज्ञानविग्रहा *Jnaana-vigrahaa*

Shloka 128.

सर्ववेदान्तसंवेद्या सत्यानन्दस्वरूपिणी
लोपामुद्राच्चिता लीलाक्ण्प्तब्रह्माण्डमण्डला॥१२८

Sarva-veda-antha-sam-vaedyaa Sathya-ananda-swa-roopinee
Loepaa-mudra-archithaa Leela-knptha-brahma-anda-mandalaa

128.

[646]She known through Upanishads – Glory,
[647]She the supreme truth and bliss – Glory,
[648]She leads to bliss and freedom – Glory,
[649]She creates universes by just play – Glory.

- 239 -

Shloka 129.

अदृश्या दृश्यरहिता विज्ञात्री वेद्यवर्जिता
योगिनी योगदा योग्या योगानन्दा युगन्धरा ॥१२९

Adr'shyaa Dr'shya-rahithaa Vijnaathree Vedya-varjjithaa
Yoeginee Yoga-daa Yoegyaa Yoega-aananda Yugandharaa

129.

[650]She who cannot be seen – Glory,
[651]She is everything see-able – Glory,
[652]She is beyond experience – Glory,
[653]To Her nothing unknown be – Glory.

- 240 -

---

[646] सर्ववेदान्तसंवेद्या Sarva-veda-antha-sam-vaedyaa
[647] सत्यानन्दस्वरूपिणी Sathya-ananda-swa-roopinee
[648] लोपामुद्राच्चिता Loepaa-mudra-archithaa
[649] लीलाक्ण्प्तब्रह्माण्डमण्डला Leela-kn'ptha-brahma-anda-mandalaa
[650] अदृश्या Adr'shyaa
[651] दृश्यरहिता Dr'shya-rahithaa
[652] विज्ञात्री Vijnaathree
[653] वेद्यवर्जिता Vedya-varjjithaa

654 She personification of Yoga – Glory,
655She grants union with divine – Glory,
She who grants of all material – Glory,
She the worldy experiences – Glory.
- 241 -

656She who is certainly worthy – Glory,
657She is bliss in divine union – Glory,
658She who the four yugas* be – Glory,
She attires in eons of time – Glory.
- 242 -

Shloka 130.

इच्छाशक्तिज्ञानशक्तिक्रियाशक्तिस्वरूपिणी
सर्वाधारा सुप्रतिष्ठा सदसद्रूपधारिणी ॥१३०

*Ich'cha-shakti-jnaana-shakti-kriya-shakti-swaroopinee
Sarva-aadhaaraa Su-prathisht'taa Sath-asath-roopa-dhaarinee*
130.

659She the desire to perform be – Glory,
She knowledge to perform be – Glory,
And She the performance be – Glory,
660 She the basis of everything – Glory.
- 243 -

---

654 योगिनी *Yoeginee*

655 योगदा *Yoga-daa*

656 योग्या *Yogyaa*

657 योगानन्दा *Yoega-aananda*

658 युगन्धरा *Yugan-dharaa; * krtha, thretha, dwaapara and kali*

659 इच्छाशक्तिज्ञानशक्तिक्रियाशक्तिस्वरूपिणी*Ich'cha-shakti-jnaana-shakti-kriya-shakti-swaroopinee*

660 सर्वाधारा *Sarva-aadhaaraa*

[661]She surely beyond time – Glory,
She the best place of stay – Glory,
[662]She the supreme truth be – Glory,
She always has truth in her – Glory.
- 244 -

Shloka 131.

अष्टमूर्त्तिरजाजैत्री लोकयात्राविधायिनी
एकाकिनी भूमरूपा निर्द्वैता द्वैतवर्जिता ॥१३१॥

*Ashta-moorthi-r-aja-jyithree Loeka-yaathraa-vidhayinee
Ekakinee Bhooma-roopa Ni-r-dwaithaa Dwaitha-varjjithaa*

131.

[663]She has eight different forms – Glory,
[664] She has won over ignorance – Glory,
[665]She who controls all the life – Glory,
[666]She who is herself and alone – Glory.
- 245 -

[667]She who is the supreme truth – Glory,
What we see, hear, understand She be,
[668] She who makes everything one – Glory,
[669]She is away from more than one – Glory.
- 246 -

---

[661] सुप्रतिष्ठा *Su-prathisht'taa*

[662] सदसद्रूपधारिणी *Sath-asath-roopa-dhaarinee*

[663] अष्टमूर्त्तिः *Ashta-moorthi:*

[664] अजाजैत्री *Aja-jaithree*

[665] लोकयात्राविधायिनी *Loeka-yaathraa-vidhayinee*

[666] एकाकिनी *Ekaakinee*

[667] भूमरूपा *Bhooma-roopa*

[668] निर्द्वैता *Ni-r-dwaithaa*

[669] द्वैतवर्जिता *Dwaitha-varjjithaa*

Shloka 132.

अन्नदा वसुदा वृद्धा ब्रह्मात्मैक्यस्वरूपिणी
बृहती ब्राह्मणी ब्राह्मी ब्रह्मानन्दा बलिप्रिया ॥१३२

*Anna-daa Vasu-daa Vr'dhaa Brahma-aathma-aikya-swa-roopinee
Br'hathee Braahmanee Braahmee Brahma-aananda Bali-priyaa*
132.

[670]She nourishment of universe – Glory,
She who is the food provider – Glory,
[671] She who gives all the wealth – Glory,
[672] She who is extremely old – Glory.
- 247 -

[673] She merges in ultimate truth – Glory,
[674]She who is exceptionally big – Glory,
[675]She is exceptionally saintly – Glory,
She is the wife of *easwar* – Glory.
- 248 -

[676]She who is the lord of worlds – Glory,
She has one aspect of Brahma – Glory,
[677]She who is the ultimate bliss – Glory,
[678]She who is fond of offerings* – Glory.
- 249 -

---

[670] अन्नदा *Anna-daa*

[671] वसुदा *Vasu-daa*

[672] वृद्धा *Vr'dhaa*

[673] ब्रह्मात्मैक्यस्वरूपिणी *Brahma-aathma-aikya-swa-roopinee*

[674] बृहती *Br'hathee*

[675] ब्राह्मणी *Braahmanee*

[676] ब्राह्मी *Braahmee*

[677] ब्रह्मानन्दा *Brahma-aananda*

[678] बलिप्रिया *Bali-priyaa; * surrender of fruits of actions*

Shloka 133.

भाषारूपा बृहल्सेना भावभावविवर्जिता
सुखाराध्या शुभकरी शोभना सुलभा गति: ॥१३३

Bhaasha-roopaa Br'hal-saenaa Bhaava-abhaava-vi-varjjithaa
Sukha-aaraadhyaa Shubha-karee Shobhana-sulabha-gathih

133.

[679]She manifests in languages – Glory,
[680]Her orders are carried out instantly,
[681]Who has no beginning or end truly,
[682]She worshipped with ease be – Glory.
- 250 -

She without any strict rules be – Glory,
[683]She bestower of blessings be – Glory,
She who does good constantly – Glory,
[684]She easily reached by path of saintly.
- 251 -

---

[679] भाषारूपा Bhaashaa-roopaa

[680] बृहल्सेना Br'hal-saenaa

[681] भावभावविवर्जिता Bhaava-abhaava-vi-varjjithaa

[682] सुखाराध्या Sukha-aaraadhyaa

[683] शुभकरी Subha-karee

[684] शोभना सुलभा गति: Shobhana-sulabhaa-gathih

Shloka 134.

राजराजेश्वरी राज्यदायिनी राज्यवल्लभा
राजत्कृपा राजपीठनिवेशितनिजाश्रिता ॥१३४

Raaja-raaja-eswaree Raajya-daayinee Raajya-vallabhaa
Raajath-kr'paa Raaja-peet'ta-nivaeshitha-nija-aashrithaa

134.

[685]She the lord for even kings be – Glory,
She lord to even the wealthiest be – Glory,
[686]She gives not only kingdoms worldly,
But Her eternal kingdom to devotees.
- 252 -

[687]She Protector of the worlds be – Glory,
[688]She who unlimited kindness be – Glory,
Her mercy shines everywhere – Glory,
[689]She gives royal placements to devotee.
- 253 -

---

[685] राजराजेश्वरी *Raaja-raaja-eswaree*

[686] राज्यदायिनी *Raajya-daayinee*

[687] राज्यवल्लभा *Raajya-vallabhaa*

[688] राजत्कृपा *Raajath-kr'paa*

[689] राजपीठनिवेशितनिजाश्रिता *Raaja-peet'ta-nivaeshitha-nija-aashrithaa*

Shloka 135.

राज्यलक्ष्मी: कोशनाथा चतुरंगबलेश्वरी
साम्राज्यदायिनी सत्यसन्धा सागरमेखला ॥१३५

Raaja-lakshmeeh Koesha-naathaa Chathu-r-anga-bala-eswaree
Saamraajya-daayinee Sathya-sandhaa Saagara-maekhalaa

135.

[690]She world of wealth and glory be,
[691]She the lord of all treasures – Glory,
[692]She the leader of four fold armies*,
[693]She makes a king of Her devotee.
- 254 -

[694]She promises to be truthful actually,
She who is truthful eternally – Glory,
[695]She the earth with oceans – Glory,
She the earth surrounded by sea be.
- 255 -

---

[690] राज्यलक्ष्मी: *Raajya-lakshmih*

[691] कोशनाथा *Koesha-naat'thaa*

[692] चतुरंगबलेश्वरी *Chathu-r-anga-bala-eswaree; * mind, brain, thought and ego*

[693] साम्राज्यदायिनी *Saamraajya-daayinee*

[694] सत्यसन्धा *Sathya-sandhaa*

[695] सागरमेखला *Saagara-maekhalaa*

श्री ललिता सहस्रनाम

Shloka 136.

दीक्षिता दैत्यशमनी सर्व्वलोकवशंकरी
सर्व्वार्त्थदात्री सावित्री सच्चिदानन्दरूपिणी ॥१३६

Deekshitha Daithya-shamanee Sarva-loeka-vasam-karee
Sarva-art'tha-daathree Saavithree Sath-chith-aananda-roopinee
                                                          136.

[696]She with great perseverance be,
She destroys sins in the devotee,
[697]She who destroys evil – Glory,
She controls anti gods – Glory.
- 256 -

[698]She who attracts all worlds – Glory,
[699]She who grants all wealth to the devotee
She grants the desires* to devotee,
[700]She the light of all life be – Glory,
[701]She who ultimate bliss be – Glory.
- 257 -

---

[696] *दीक्षिता Deekshithaa*

[697] *दैत्यशमनी Daithya-shamanee*

[698] *सर्व्वलोकवशंकरी Sarva-loeka-vasham-karee*

[699] *सर्व्वार्त्थदात्री Sarva-art'tha-daathree; * of righteousness, wealth, desires and also liberation from the cycle of births and death*

[700] *सावित्री Saavithree*

[701] *सच्चिदानन्दरूपिणी Sath-chith-aananda-roopinee*

8th Shathaka

Shloka 137.

देशकालापरिच्छिन्ना सर्व्वगा सर्व्वमोहिनी
सरस्वती शास्त्रमयी गुहांबा गुह्यरूपिणी ॥१३७

Deasa-kaala-aparich'chinna Sarva-gaa Sarva-moehinee
Saraswathee Shastramayee Guha-ambaa Guhya-roopinee

137.

[702]She not measured in space, time be,
[703]She who is but every where – Glory,
[704]She who attracts every thing – Glory,
[705]She the supreme knowledge – Glory.
- 258 -

[706]She manifested in all scriptures – Glory,
She goddess of knowledge be – Glory,
[707]She the meaning of sciences – Glory,
[708]Her form is hidden from all – Glory.
- 259 -

---

[702] देशकालापरिच्छिन्ना Deasa-kaala-aparich'chinna

[703] सर्व्वगा Sarva-gaa

[704] सर्वमोहिनी Sarva-moehinee

[705] सरस्वती Saraswathee

[706] शास्त्रमयी Shaastramayee

[707] गुहांबा Guha-ambaa

[708] गुह्यरूपिणी Guhya-roopinee

श्री ललिता सहस्रनाम

Shloka 138.

सर्वोपादिविनिर्म्मुक्ता सदाशिवपतिव्रता
संप्रदायेश्वरी साध्वी गुरुमण्डलरूपिणी ॥१३८

Sarva-o-upaadi-vi-ni-r-muktaa Sadaa-shiva-pathi-vrathaa
Sampradaaya-eswaree Saadhu-ee Guru-mandala-roopinee
138.

[709]She free from all descriptions – Glory,
She who cannot be described – Glory,
[710]She on whom supreme truth be – Glory,
She devoted wife of Lord Shiv – Glory.
- 260 -

[711] She lord to teacher-student hierarchy,
[712]She in virtue, a balanced mind-state be,
[713]From Her universe came to be – Glory,
[714]She universe round teachers – Glory.
- 261 -

---

[709] सर्वोपादिविनिर्म्मुक्ता *Sarva--o-upaadi-vi-ni-r-muktaa*

[710] सदाशिवपतिव्रता *Sadaa-shiva-pathi-vrathaa*

[711] संप्रदायेश्वरी *Sampradaaya-eswaree*

[712] साधु *Saadhu*

[713] ई *Ee*

[714] गुरुमण्डलरूपिणी *Guru-mandala-roopinee*

Shloka 139.

कुलोत्तीर्णा भगाराध्या माया मधुमती मही
गणाम्बा गुह्यकाराध्या कोमलांगी गुरुप्रिया ॥१३९

Kula-o-ut'theernnaa Bhaga-aaraadhyaa Maayaa Madhu-mathee Mahee
Gana-amba Guhyakaa-aaradhyaa Komala-angee Guru-priyaa
139.

[715]She who beyond the mind – Glory,
She who beyond senses – Glory,
[716]She worshiped as the sun – Glory,
[717]She who creates illusion – Glory.
- 262 -

She who is the illusion – Glory,
[718]She the essence of life – Glory,
She trance stage in yoga – Glory,
[719]She who but be the earth – Glory.
- 263 -

[720]The mother of every thing – Glory,
[721]She adored in secret places – Glory,
[722]She with a very soft body – Glory,
[723]She who teachers love – Glory.
- 264 -

---

[715] कुलोत्तीर्णा Kula-o-ut'theernnaa

[716] भगाराध्या Bhaga-aaraadhyaa

[717] माया Maayaa

[718] मधुमती Madhu-mathee

[719] मही Mahee

[720] गणाम्बा Gana-amba

[721] गुह्यकाराध्या Guhyaka-aaradhyaa

[722] कोमलांगी Komala-angee

[723] गुरुप्रिया Guru-priyaa

Shloka 140.

स्वतन्त्रा सर्व्वतन्त्रेशी दक्षीणामूर्त्तिरूपिणी

सनकादिसमाराध्या शिवज्ञानप्रदायिनी ॥१४०

Swa-thanthraa Sarva-thanthra-esee Dakshina-moorthy-roopinee
Sanaka-aadi-sama-aaraadhya Shiva-jnaana-pradaayinee

140.

[724]She free of limitations and rules be,
She who is independent – Glory,
[725]She the lord of all *thanthras** – Glory,
She who gives power to all thanthras.
- 265 -

[726]She worshiped *as dakshina-moorthy*,
She teacher form of Shiv – Glory,
[727]She worshipped by great Rishis,
[728]She gives knowledge of God – Glory.
- 266 -

Shloka 141.

चित्कलाऽऽनन्दकलिका प्रेमरूपा प्रियंकरी

नामपारायणप्रीता नन्दिविद्या नटेश्वरी ॥१४१

Chith-kalaa Ananda-kalikaa Prema-roopaa Priyam-karee
Naama-paarayana-preethaa Nandi-vidyaa Nada-eeswaree

141.

[729]She micro essence of all – Glory,
She is micro power within – Glory,
[730] She happiness in beings – Glory,
[731] She is the form of love – Glory.
- 267 -

---

[724] स्वतन्त्रा *Swa-thanthraa*

[725] सर्व्वतन्त्रेशी *Sarva-thanthra-esee; * tricks to attain God*

[726] दक्षीणामूर्त्तिरूपिणी *Dakshina-moorthy-roopinee*

[727] सनकादिसमाराध्या *Sanaka-aadi-sama-aaraadhya*

[728] शिवज्ञानप्रदायिनी *Shiva-jnaana-pradayinee*

[729] चित्कला *Chith-kalaa*

[730] आनन्दकलिका *Ananda-kalikaa*

[731] प्रेमरूपा *Prema-roopaa*

[732] She who does what is liked – Glory,
[733] She likes being addressed sincerely,
[734] She is the sincere prayer of Nandi,
[735] She the goddess of dance – Glory.
- 268 -

Shloka 142.

मिथ्या जगदधिष्ठाना मुक्तिदा मुक्तिरूपिणी
लास्यप्रिया लयकरी लज्जा रंभादिवन्तिता ॥१४२

Mit'thyaa Jagath-adhisht'taanaa Mukti-daa Mukti-roopinee
Laasya-priya Laya-karee Lajjaa Rambha-aadi-vandithaa

142.

[736] She who is luck in illusion – Glory,
[737] She who gives redemption – Glory,
[738] She who is the redemption – Glory,
[739] She fond of universal dance – Glory.
- 269 -

[740] In Her all do merge finally – Glory,
She bridge between dance, music be,
[741] She the shame in acts unholy that be,
[742] She deified by celestial dancers holy.
- 270 -

---

[732] प्रियंकरी *Priyam-karee*
[733] नामपारायणप्रीता *Naama-paarayana-preethaa*
[734] नन्दिविद्या *Nandi-vidyaa*
[735] नटेश्वरी *Nada-eeswaree*
[736] मिथ्या जगदधिष्ठाना *Mit'thyaa Jagath-adhisht'taanaa*
[737] मुक्तिदा *Mukti-daa*
[738] मुक्तिरूपिणी *Mukti-roopinee*
[739] लास्यप्रिया *Laasya-priya*
[740] लयकरी *Laya-karee*
[741] लज्जा *Lajjaa*
[742] रंभादिवन्तिता *Rambha-aadi-vandithaa*

Shloka 143.

भवदावसुधावृष्टी: पापारण्यदवानला
दौर्भाग्यतूलवातूला जराध्वान्तरविप्रभा ॥१४३

Bhava-daava-sudha-vr'shtih Paapa-aaranya-dava-anala
Dourbhaagya-thoola-vaathoola Jaraa-dwaantha-ravi-prabhaa
143.

[743]She who is the cooling nectar – Glory,
To the problems of life that as fire be,
[744]She the fire that does destroys fully,
The forest of sins and evil – all Glory.
- 271 -

[745]She is the whirl-wind that carries,
Cotton bundles of misfortune – Glory,
[746]She the sun light ray to darkness be,
That nips darkness of age – Glory
- 272 -

Shloka 144.

भाग्याब्धिचन्द्रिका भक्तचित्तकेकिघनाघना
रोगपर्व्वतदंभोलि: मृत्युदारुकुठारिका ॥१४४

Bhaagya-abdhi-chandrikaa Bhakta-chit'tha-kaeki--ghana-ghanaa
Roega-parvatha-damboli-r-mr'thyu-daaru-kut'taarikaa
144.

[747]She the light of the full moon be,
To ocean of the tides of luck – Glory,
[748]She as black-clouds to peacocks be,
Makes them dance in glee – devotees.
- 273 -

---

[743] भवदावसुधावृष्टी: *Bhava-daava-sudhaa-vr'shtih*

[744] पापारण्यदवानला *Paapa-aaranya-dava-anala*

[745] दौर्भाग्यतूलवातूला *Dourbhaagya-thoola-vaathoola*

[746] जराध्वान्तरविप्रभा *Jaraa-dwaantha-ravi-prabhaa*

[747] भाग्याब्धिचन्द्रिका *Bhaagya-abdhi-chandrikaa*

[748] भक्तचित्तकेकिघनाघना *Bhakta-chit'tha-kaeki-ghana-ghanaa*

[749]She the weapon that cut through easily,
Mountains of ill-health, diseases – Glory,
[750]She the axe that can cut but effortlessly,
The tree that embodiment of death but be.
- 274 -

Shloka 145.

महेश्वरी महाकाली महाग्रासा महाशना

अपर्णा चण्डिका चण्डमुण्डासुरनिषूदिनी॥१४५

*Maha-eeswaree Maha-kaalee Maha-graasaa Maha-asanaa
Aparnnaa Chandikaa Chanda-munda-asura-nishoodinee*

145.

[751] She the greatest goddess – Glory,
[752]She who great and beyond time be,
She who destroys the world – Glory,
[753]She grasps all at destruction finally.
- 275 -

[754]She who eat up everything – Glory,
[755]She who debt free of all be – Glory,
[756]She burns of anger to evil severely,
[757]She the destroyer of evil* – Glory.
- 276 -

---

[749] रोगपर्व्वतदंभोलिः *Roega-parvatha-dambolih*

[750] मृत्युदारुकुठारिका *Mr'thyu-daaru-kut'taarikaa*

[751] महेश्वरी *Maha-eeswaree*

[752] महाकाली *Maha-kaalee*

[753] महाग्रासा *Maha-graasaa*

[754] महाशना *Maha-ashanaa*

[755] अपर्णा *Aparnnaa*

[756] चण्डिका *Chandikaa*

[757] चण्डमुण्डासुरनिषूदिनी *Chanda-munda-asura-nishoodinee; * as asuras Chanda and Munda*

श्री ललिता सहस्रनाम

Shloka 146.

क्षाराक्षरात्मिका सर्व्वलोकेशी विश्वधारिणी
त्रिवर्ग्गदात्री सुभगा त्र्यंबिका त्रिगुणात्मिका ॥१४६

Kshara-akshara-aathmikaa Sarva-loeka-esi Vishwa-dhaarinee
Thri-varga-daathree Subhagaa Thri-ambikaa Thri-guna-aathmikaa
146.

[758]She destructible and indestructible – Glory,
[759]She who is the lord of all worlds – Glory,
[760]She supports the entire universe – Glory,
She who the bearer of Glaxies does be.
- 277 -

[761]She who grants of three boons* – Glory,
[762] She who is pleasing to look at – Glory,
[763]She who has three big eyes* – Glory,
[764]She who has three impulses* – Glory.
- 278 -

---

[758] क्षाराक्षरात्मिका *Kshara-akshara-aathmikaa*

[759] सर्व्वलोकेशी *Sarva-loeka-esi*

[760] विश्वधारिणी *Vishwa-dhaarinee*

[761] त्रिवर्ग्गदात्री *Thri-varga-daathree;*
   * righteousness, wealth and desires or dharma, assets and pleasure

[762] सुभगा *Subhagaa*

[763] त्र्यंबिका *Thri-ambikaa;* * the sun, moon and fire

[764] त्रिगुणात्मिका *Thri-guna-aathmikaa;* * saintliness (satwa), disturbance (rajas) and
ignorance (tamas) or three gunas viz., Thamo (Kali), Rajo (Dhurga) and Sathva
(Parvathy)" – Glory.

Shloka 147.

स्वर्गापवर्गदा शुद्धा जापापुष्पनिभाकृति:
ओजोवती द्वितिधरा यज्ञरूपा प्रियव्रता ॥१४७

Swarga-apa-varga-daa Shudhaa Japa-pushpa-nibha-aakr'thih
Oeja-o-vathee Dwithi-dharaa Yajna-roopa Priya-vrathaa

147.

765 She gives heaven, its path – Glory,
She grants freedom from rebirth – Glory,
766 She who is pure and clean – Glory,
767 She glows as hibiscus flower – Glory.
- 279 -

768 She who is filled with vigour – Glory,
769 She who is source of all light – Glory,
770 She peaceful co-existence be – Glory,
771 She who likes true penances – Glory.
- 280 -

---

765 स्वर्गापवर्गदा *Swarga-apa-varga-daa*

766 शुद्धा *Shudhaa*

767 जापापुष्पनिभाकृति: *Japaa-pushpa-nibha-aakr'thih*

768 ओजोवती *Oeja-o-vathee*

769 द्वितिधरा *Dwithi-dharaa*

770 यज्ञरूपा *Yajna-roopa*

771 प्रियव्रता *Priya-vrathaa*

Shloka 148.

दुराराध्या दूराधर्षा पाटलीकुसुमप्रिया
महती मेरुनिलया मन्दारकुसुमप्रिया॥१४८

Du-r-aaradhyaa Du-r-aadarshaa Paatalee-kusuma-priyaa
Mahathee Maeru-nilayaa Mandaara-kusuma-priyaa

148.

[772]She extremely difficult to worship – Glory,
She worshipped by the good and saintly,
[773]She who cannot be influenced easily,
She not won by evil certainly – Glory.
- 281 -

[774]She likes the buds of Patali tree – Glory,
[775]She the greatest of all does be – Glory,
[776]She exists as unawakened *'kundalini'*,
[777] She likes buds of Mandhara tree – Glory,
- 282 -

---

[772] *दुराराध्या Du-r-aaradhyaa*

[773] *दूराधर्षा Duraadharshaa*

[774] *पाटलीकुसुमप्रिया Paatalee-kusuma-priyaa*

[775] *महती Mahathee*

[776] *मेरुनिलया Maeru-nilayaa; * the light of life, unknown to ordinary human being*

[777] *मन्दारकुसुमप्रिया Mandaara-kusuma-priyaa*

Shloka 149.

वीराराध्या विराड्रूपा विरजा विश्वतोमुखी
प्रत्यग्रूपा पराकाशा प्राणदा प्राणरूपिणी ॥१४९॥

*Veera-aaraadhyaaa Viraad-roopaa Vi-rajaa Vishwatha-o-mukhee
Prathyak-roopaa Para-aakaashaa Praana-daa Praana-roopinee
149.*

[778] She is worshipped by heroes – Glory,
[779] She who has a universal look – Glory,
[780] She who has not any blemish – Glory,
[781] She sees through every eye – Glory.
- 283 -

[782] She be seen by looking within – Glory,
[783] She who the life's true light be – Glory,
[784] She who gives and takes life – Glory,
[785] She who is the very life soul – Glory.
- 284 -

---

[778] वीराराध्या *Veera-aaraadhyaaa*

[779] विराड्रूपा *Viraad-roopaa;*

[780] विरजा *Vi-rajaa*

[781] विश्वतोमुखी *Vishwatha-o-mukhee*

[782] प्रत्यग्रूपा *Prathyak-roopaa*

[783] पराकाशा *Para-aakaashaa*

[784] प्राणदा *Praana-daa*

[785] प्राणरूपिणी *Praana-roopinee*

श्री ललिता सहस्रनाम

Shloka 150.

मात्तार्ण्डभैरवाराध्या मन्त्रिणीन्यस्तराज्यधूः
त्रिपुरेशी जयत्सेना निस्त्रैगुण्या परापरा ॥१५०

Maart'thaanda-bhairava-aaraadhyaa Manthrinee-nyastha-raajya-dhooh
Thri-pura-esi Jayath-saenaa Ni-s-thri-gunyaa Paraa-aparaa

150.

[786]She whose hearts always in truth be,
[787]She in complete surrender of mind be,
[788]She lord of wakefulness, dream, sleep be,
[789]She ever victorious over evil forces be.
- 285 -

She has victory over desires, anger fully,
[790]She free of the three natural qualities*,
She above these three qualities does be,
[791] She who is outside and inside – Glory.
- 286 -

---

[786] मात्तार्ण्डभैरवाराध्या *Maart'thaanda-bhairava-aaraadhyaa*

[787] मन्त्रिणीन्यस्तराज्यधू *Manthrinee-nyastha-raajya-dhooh*

[788] त्रिपुरेशी *Thri-pura-esi*

[789] जयत्सेना *Jayath-saenaa; * of satwa-raja-s-tama*

[790] निस्त्रैगुण्या *Ni-s-thri-gunyaa*

[791] परापरा *Paraa-aparaa*

Shloka 151.

सत्यज्ञानानन्दरूपा सामरस्यपरायणा

कपर्दिनी कलामाला कामधुक् कामरूपिणी ॥१५१

sathya-jnaana-ananda-roopaa saama-rasya-paraayanaa
Kaparddinee Kalaa-maalaa-kaama-duk kaama-roopinee

151.

[792]She supreme knowledge, bliss be,
"She is truth, awareness, bliss – Glory,
[793]She who in full surrender of senses be,
[794] She the wife of Kapardhi truly – Glory.
- 287 -

She supports entire universe – Glory,
[795] She who wears arts as garlands – Glory,
[796]She who fulfills all desires of the devotee,
[797]She desire in tune with righteousness be,
- 288 -

---

[792] सत्यज्ञानानन्दरूपा *Sathya-jnaana-ananda-roopaa*

[793] सामरस्यपरायणा *Saama-rasya-paraayanaa*

[794] कपर्दिनी *Kaparddinee*

[795] कलामाला *Kalaa-maalaa*

[796] कामधुक् *Kaama-dhuk*

[797] कामरूपिणी *Kaama-roopinee*

Shloka 152.

कलानिधि: काव्यकला रसज्ञा रसशेवधि:
पुष्टा पुरातना पूज्या पुष्करा पुष्करेक्षणा ॥१५२

*Kalaa-nidhih Kaavya-kalaa Rasa-jnaa Rasa-shaevadhih
Pushtaa Puraathanaa Poojyaa Push-karaa Pushka-r-eekshanaa*
                                                    152.

[798]She the life treasure in the physical body
She who is the treasure of arts – Glory,
[799]She the great poetry of great poets be,
She who is the art of writing – Glory.
- 289 -

[800]She who appreciates all arts – Glory,
[801]She essence of everything – Glory,
[802]She is worshipped by all – Glory,
[803]She who is very ancient – Glory.
- 290 -

[804]She who worthy of worship be,
[805]She who gives exuberance – Glory,
[806]Her eyes like the petals of lotus be,
They sees all yet unattached – Glory.
- 291 -

---

[798] कलानिधि: *Kalaa-nidhih*

[799] काव्यकला *Kaavya-kalaa*

[800] रसज्ञा *Rasa-jnaa*

[801] रसशेवधि: *Rasa-shaevathih*

[802] पुष्टा *Pushtaa*

[803] पुरातना *Puraathanaa*

[804] पूज्या *Poojyaa*

[805] पुष्करा *Push-karaa*

[806] पुष्करेक्षणा *Pushkara-eekshanaa*

9th Shathaka

Shloka 153.

परंज्योति: परंधाम परमाणु: परात्परा
पाशहस्ता पाशहन्त्री परमन्त्रविभेदिनी॥१५

Param-jyothih Param-dhaama Parama-anuh Paraath-paraa
Paasha-hasthaa Paasha-hanthree Para-manthra-vibhaedinee
153.

[807] She who is the ultimate light – Glory,
[808] She who is the destination – Glory,
[809] She who is the ultimate atom – Glory,
[810] She is greater than greatest – Glory.
- 292 -

She who is better than the best – Glory,
[811] She who has rope in her hand – Glory,
[812] She who cuts off attachment – Glory,
[813] She destroys effect of spells – Glory.
- 293 -

---

[807] परंज्योति: *Param-jyothih*

[808] परंधाम *Param-dhaama*

[809] परमाणु: *Parama-anuh*

[810] परात्परा *Paraath-paraa*

[811] पाशहस्ता *Paasha-hasthaa*

[812] पाशहन्त्री *Paasha-hanthree*

[813] परमन्त्रविभेदिनी *Para-manthra-vibhaedinee*

Shloka 154.

मूर्त्ताऽमूर्त्ताऽनित्यतृप्ता मुनिमानसहंसिका
सत्यव्रता सत्यरूपा सर्व्वान्तर्य्यामिणी सती ॥१५४

Moorthaa-amoorthaa Anithya-tr'pthaa Muni-maanasa-hamsikaa
Sathya-vrathaa Sathya-roopaa Sarva-anthara-yaaminee Sathee
154.

[814] She who has a form – Glory,
[815] She who is formless – Glory,
[816] She is fond of devotion – Glory,
[817] She the swan in mind of devotee.
- 294 -

[818] She resolved to speak truth – Glory,
[819] She who is the true form – Glory,
[820] She is within everything – Glory,
[821] She who is the real truth – Glory.
- 295 -

---

[814] मूर्त्ता *Moorthaa*

[815] अमूर्त्ता *Amoorthaa*

[816] अनित्यतृप्ता *Anithya-tr'pthaa*

[817] मुनिमानसहंसिका *Muni-maana-sahamsikaa*

[818] सत्यव्रता *Sathya-vrathaa*

[819] सत्यरूपा *Sathya-roopaa*

[820] सर्व्वान्तर्य्यामिणी *Sarva-antha-r-yaaminee*

[821] सती *Sathee*

Shloka 155.

ब्रह्माणी ब्रह्मजननी बहुरूपा बुधाच्चिता
प्रसवित्रीप्रचण्डाऽऽज्ञा प्रतिष्ठा प्रकटाकृतिः ॥१५५

*Brahmaanee Brahma-jananee Bahu-roopaa Budha-archithaa
Prasavithree Pra-chandaa-aajnaa Prathishtaa Prakata-akrithih*

155.

[822]She the basis for universe – Glory,
She strength behind creator – Glory,
[823]She supreme truth, destination be,
She who is the real creator – Glory.
- 296 -

[824]She who is the Mother – Glory,
[825]She in unlimited forms be – Glory,
She who has several forms – Glory,
[826] She worshipped by enlightened – Glory.
- 297 -

[827] She gives birth to everything – Glory,
[828]She who has great anger – Glory,
She controls all the angry forces fully,
[829]She gives directions, guidance – Glory.
- 298 -

---

[822] ब्रह्माणी *Brahmaanee*

[823] ब्रह्म *Brahma*

[824] जननी *Jananee*

[825] बहुरूपा *Bahu-roopaa*

[826] बुधाच्चिता *Budha-archithaa*

[827] प्रसवित्री *Prasavithree*

[828] प्रचण्डा *Pra-chandaa*

[829] आज्ञा *Aajnaa*

She who is the true order – Glory,
830She supports the universe – Glory,
She who has been installed – Glory,
831 She who is visible clearly – Glory.
- 299 -

Shloka 156.

प्राणेश्वरी प्राणदात्री पञ्चाशत्पीठरूपिणी

विश्रृङ्गला विविक्तस्था वीरमाता वियत्प्रसूः ॥१५६

Praana-eswaree Praana-daathree Panchaa-shath-peet'ta-roopinee
Vi-shr'ngalaa Viviktha-st'thaa Veera-maathaa Viyath-prasooh

156.

832She is goddess to soul – Glory,
833She is the life of the soul – Glory,
834She the basis of alphabets – Glory,
835 She who is not chained – Glory.
- 300 -

She not bonded by actions – Glory,
836 She who is in lonely places – Glory,
837 She brave mother does be – Glory,
838She five basic elements* be – Glory.
- 301 -

---

830 प्रतिष्ठा *Prathishtaa*

831 प्रकटाकृतिः *Prakata-akrithih*

832 प्राणेश्वरी *Praana-eswaree*

833 प्राणदात्री *Praana-daathree*

834 पञ्चाशत्पीठरूपिणी *Panchaa-shath-peet'ta-roopinee*

835 विश्रृङ्गला *Vi-shr'ngalaa*

836 विविक्तस्था *Viviktha-st'thaa*

837 वीरमाता *Veera-maathaa*

838 वियत्प्रसू *Viyath-prasooh; * aakasha-vaayu-r agni-r-aapa-o-bhoomi*

Shloka 157.

मुकुन्दा मुक्तिनिलया मूलविग्रहरूपिणी
भावज्ञा भवरोगघ्नी भवचक्रप्रवर्त्तिनी ॥१५७

Mukundaa Mukthi-nilayaa Moola-vigraha-roopinee
Bhaava-jnaa Bhava-roga-ghnee Bhava-chakra-pravart'thinee

157.

[839]She who gives redemption – Glory,
[840]She the seat of redemption – Glory,
[841]She the basis for everything – Glory,
She who is the basic statue – Glory.
- 302 -

[842]She fathoms wishes, thoughts – Glory,
[843]She destroys sorrows of life – Glory,
She who cures the sin of birth – Glory,
[844]She rotates the wheel of birth – Glory.
- 303 -

---

[839] मुकुन्दा *Mukundaa*

[840] मुक्तिनिलया *Mukthi-nilayaa*

[841] मूलविग्रहरूपिणी *Moola-vigraha-roopinee*

[842] भावज्ञा *Bhaava-jnaa*

[843] भवरोगघ्नी *Bhava-roga-gnee*

[844] भवचक्रप्रवर्त्तिनी *Bhava-chakra-pravart'thinee*

Shloka 158.

छन्दसारा शास्त्रसारा मन्त्रसारातलोदरी
उदारकीर्त्तिरुद्दामवैभवा वर्णरूपिणी॥१५८

Chanda-saaraa Shastra-saaraa Manthra-saaraa-athala-o-udara
Udaara-keerthi-r-ud'daama-vaibhavaa Varna-roopinee

158.

[845]She is the meaning of Vedas – Glory,
[846]She the meaning of Puranas – Glory,
[847]She the essence of all mantras be,
[848] She who has a small belly – Glory.
- 304 -

[849] She has wide and tall fame – Glory,
She grants fame to her devotees,
[850] She has immeasurable fame – Glory,
[851]She alphabets embodiment – Glory.
- 305 -

---

[845] छन्दसारा *Chandah saaraa*

[846] शास्त्रसारा *Shastra-saaraa*

[847] मन्त्रसारा *Manthra-saaraa*

[848] अतलोदरी *Athala-o-udare*

[849] उदारकीर्ति *Udaara-keerthi*

[850] उद्दामवैभवा *Ud'daama-vaibhavaa*

[851] वर्णरूपिणी *Varnna-roopinee*

Shloka 159.

जन्ममृत्युजरातप्तजनविश्रान्तिदायिनी
सर्वोपनिषदुद्घुष्टा शान्त्यतीतकलात्मिका ॥१५९

Janma-mr'thya-jaraa-thaptha-jana-vishraanthi-daayinee
Sarva-o-upanishad-udghushtaa Shaanthi-atheetha-kala-athmikaa

159.

[852]She the cure of all illness be,
Of birth, death and aging – Glory,
[853]She loudly stated by scriptures be,
[854]She beyond total peace, tranquility.
- 306 -

Shloka 160.

गंभीरा गगनान्तस्था गर्विता गानलोलुपा
कल्पनारहिता काष्ठाऽकान्ता कान्तार्द्धविग्रहा ॥१६०

Gambheera Gagana-antha-st'thaa Garvvithaa Gaana-loelupaa
Kalpanaa-rahithaa Kaashtaa Aka-anthaa kantha-ardha-vigrahaa

160.

[855] Her depth not measureable be,
[856] She is situated in the sky – Glory,
[857] She very proud of Her acts – Glory,
[858] She likes devotional songs – Glory.
- 307 -

---

[852] जन्ममृत्युजरातप्तजनविश्रान्तिदायिनी *Janma-mr'thyu-jaraa-thaptha-jana-vishraanthi-daayinee*

[853] सर्वोपनिषदुद्घुष्टा *Sarva-o-upanishad-udghushtaa*

[854] शान्त्यतीतकलात्मिका *Shaanthi-atheetha-kala-athmikaa*

[855] गंभीरा *Gambheera*

[856] गगनान्तस्था *Gagana-antha-st'thaa*

[857] गर्विता *Garvvithaa*

[858] गानलोलुपा *Gaana-loelupaa*

श्री ललिता सहस्रनाम

⁸⁵⁹ She is beyond imagination – Glory,
⁸⁶⁰She is the ultimate state – Glory,
⁸⁶¹ She who removes all sins – Glory,
⁸⁶²She ardha-naree-eeswara deity be.
- 308 -

Shloka 161.

कार्य्यकारणनिर्म्मुक्ता कामकेलितरंगिता

कनत्कनकताटङ्का लीलाविग्रहधारिणी ॥१६१

*Kaarya-kaarana-ni-r-muktaa Kaama-kaeli-tharangithaa
Kanath-kanaka-thaatangaa Leela-vigraha-dhaarinee*

161.

⁸⁶³ She beyond action and the cause – Glory,
⁸⁶⁴ She joy waves in divine union be – Glory,
⁸⁶⁵ She wears glitzy golden ear studs – Glory,
⁸⁶⁶She dons several forms as play – Glory.
- 309 -

---

⁸⁵⁹ कल्पनारहिता *Kalpanaa-rahithaa*

⁸⁶⁰ काष्ठा *Kaashtaa*

⁸⁶¹ अकान्ता *Aka-anthaa*

⁸⁶² कान्तार्द्धविग्रहा *Kantha-ardha-vigrahaa*

⁸⁶³ कार्य्यकारणनिर्म्मुक्ता *Kaarya-kaarana-ni-r-muktaa*

⁸⁶⁴ कामकेलितरंगिता *Kaama-kaeli-tharangithaa*

⁸⁶⁵ कनत्कनकताटङ्का *Kanath-kanaka-thaatangaa*

⁸⁶⁶ लीलाविग्रहधारिणी *Leela-vigraha-dhaarinee*

Shloka 162.

अजा क्षयविनिर्म्मुक्ता मुग्द्धा क्षिप्रप्रसादिनी
अन्तर्म्मुखसमाराध्या बहिर्म्मुखसुदुर्ल्लभा ॥१६२

Ajaa Kshaya-vi-ni-r-muktaa Mugdhaa Kshipra-prasaadinee
Antha-r-mukha-sama-aaradhyaa Bahi-r-mukha-su-du-r-labhaa

162.

[867]She who does not have birth – Glory,
[868]She who without death, destruction be
She who knows not any death – Glory,
[869] She who is uniquely beautiful – Glory.

- 310 -

[870] She who is pleased very quickly – Glory,
[871] She revered by internal thoughts – Glory,
[872]She unattainable to desire chasers worldly,
She attained by external prayers – Glory.

- 311 -

---

[867] अजा *Ajaa*

[868] क्षयविनिर्म्मुक्ता *Kshaya-vi-ni-r-muktaa*

[869] मुग्द्धा *Mugdhaa*

[870] क्षिप्रप्रसादिनी *Kshipra-prasaadinee*

[871] अन्तर्म्मुखसमाराध्या *Antha-r-mukha-sama-aaradhyaa*

[872] बहिर्म्मुखसुदुर्ल्लभा *Bahi-r-mukha-su-du-r-labhaa*

श्री ललिता सहस्रनाम

Shloka 163.

त्रयी त्रिवर्गनिलया त्रिस्था त्रिपुरमालिनी
निरामया निरालंबा स्वात्मारामा सुधासृति: ॥१६३

Thrayee Thri-varga-nilayaa Thri-st'thaa Thri-pura-maalinee
Ni-r-aamayaa Ni-r-aalambaa Swa-aathma-raama Sudhaa-sr'thih
163.

[873] She the form of three Vedas* – Glory,
[874] She present in three aspects – Glory,
[875] She in three phases* of life – Glory,
[876] She adored as centre of Chakra Sri.
- 312 -

[877] She who is without illness – Glory,
[878] She not depend on anything be,
[879] She enjoys within herself – Glory,
[880] She who is rain of nectar – Glory.
- 313 -

---

[873] त्रयी *Thrayee; * Rig, yajur and sama*

[874] त्रिवर्गनिलया *Thri-varga-nilayaa; * of self, assets and pleasure*

[875] त्रिस्था *Thri-st'thaa; righteousness, wealth and desires or wakefulness, dream and sleep or past, present and future*

[876] त्रिपुरमालिनी *Thri-pura-maalinee*

[877] निरामया *Ni-r-aamayaa*

[878] निरालंबा *Ni-r-aalambaa*

[879] स्वात्मारामा *Swa-aathma-raamaa*

[880] सुधासृति: *Sudhaa-sr'thih*

Shloka 164.

संसारपङ्कनिर्म्मग्नसमुद्धरणपण्डिता
यज्ञप्रिया यज्ञकर्त्री यजमानस्वरूपिणी ॥१६४

Samsaara-panka-ni-r-magna-sam-uddharana-pandithaa
Yajna-priyaa Yajna-karthree Yajamaana-swa-roopinee

164.

[881]She saves from evil marsh of life dirty,
[882]She who likes fire sacrifice – Glory,
[883]She carries out fire sacrifice – Glory,
[884]She performs divine offerings truly.
- 314 -

Shloka 165.

धर्म्माधारा धनाद्ध्यक्षा धनधान्यविवर्द्धिनी
विप्रप्रिया विप्ररूपा विश्वभ्रमणकारिणी ॥१६५

Dharma-aadhaaraa Dhana-adhyakshaa Dhana-dhaanya-vivardhinee
Vipra-priyaa Vipra-roopaa Vishwa-bhramana-kaarinee

165.

[885]She the basis of rightful action – Glory,
She pours out righteousness – Glory,
[886]She who presides over wealth – Glory,
[887]She makes wealth, grain to grow – Glory.
- 315 -

---

[881] संसारपङ्कनिर्म्मग्नसमुद्धरणपण्डिता Samsaara-panka-ni-r-magna-sam-uddharana-pandithaa
[882] यज्ञप्रिया Yajna-priyaa
[883] यज्ञकर्त्री Yajna-karthree
[884] यजमानस्वरूपिणी Yajamaana-swa-roopaa
[885] धर्म्माधारा Dharma-aadhaaraa
[886] धनाद्ध्यक्षा Dhana-adhyakshaa
[887] धनधान्यविवर्द्धिनी Dhana-dhaanya-vivardhinee

She is extremely dear to the wise – Glory,
[888]She likes those who learn Vedas – Glory,
[889]She is the deep learner of Vedas – Glory,
[890]She makes the universe rotate – Glory.
- 316 -

Shloka 166.

विश्वग्रासा विद्रुमाभा वैष्णवी विष्णुरूपिणी
अयोनिर्य्योंनिनिलया कूटस्था कुलरूपिणी ॥१६६

Vishwa-graasaa Vidruma-abhaa Vaishnavee Vishnu-roopinee
Ayoni-r-yoni-nilayaa Kootast'thaa Kula-rooopinee

166.

[891]She grasps the world aiding – Glory,
[892]She who has luster of coral – Glory,
[893]She is the power of Vishnu – Glory,
[894]She who is the Lord Vishnu – Glory.
- 317 -

[895] She has no cause nor is born – Glory,
[896]She cause and source of all – Glory,
[897]She who is eternally stable – Glory,
[898]She personification of culture – Glory.
- 318 -

---

[888] विप्रप्रिया *Vipra-priyaa*

[889] विप्ररूपा *Vipra-roopaa*

[890] विश्वभ्रमणकारिणी *Vishwa-bhramana-kaarinee*

[891] विश्वग्रासा *Vishwa-graasaa*

[892] विद्रुमाभा *Vidruma-abhaa*

[893] वैष्णवी *Vaishnavee*

[894] विष्णुरूपिणी *Vishnu-roopinee*

[895] अयोनि *A-yoni*

[896] योनिनिलया *Yoni-nilayaa*

[897] कूटस्था *Kootast'thaa*

[898] कुलरूपिणी *Kula-roopinee*

Shloka 167.

वीरगोष्ठीप्रिया वीरा नैष्कम्म्या नादरूपिणी
विज्ञानकलना कल्या विदगद्धा बैन्दवासना ॥१६७

Veera-goeshtee-priyaa Veeraa Naish-karmmyaa Naada-roopinee
Vijnaana-kalanaa Kalyaa Vidagdhaa Baindava-aasanaa

167.

[899]She likes company of heroes – Glory,
[900]She who has the real valour – Glory,
[901]She is unattached to action – Glory,
[902] She who is the form of sound – Glory.
- 319 -
[903] She who makes the science – Glory,
[904] She who is expert in all arts – Glory,
[905]She who an expert in everything be,
[906]She revered as centre of Chakra Sri.
- 320 -

---

[899] वीरगोष्ठीप्रिया *Veera-goeshtee-priyaa*

[900] वीरा *Veeraa*

[901] नैष्कम्म्या *Naish-karmmyaa*

[902] नादरूपिणी *Naada-roopinee*

[903] विज्ञानकलना *Vijnaana-kalanaa*

[904] कल्या *Kalyaa*

[905] विदगद्धा *Vidagdhaa*

[906] बैन्दवासना *Baindava-aasanaa*

10th Shathaka

Shloka 168.

तत्वाधिका तत्वमयी तत्वमर्त्थस्वरूपिणी
सामगानप्रिया सौम्या सदाशिवकुटुम्बिनी ॥१६८

Tatwa-adikaa Tatwa-mayee Tat-twam-arttha-swaroopinee
Saama-gaana-priyaa Soumyaa Sadaa-shiva-kutumbinee

168.

[907] She is above all metaphysics – Glory,
[908] She who is the metaphysics – Glory,
[909] She is but you and you are that – Glory,
[910] She who likes singing of sama* – Glory.
- 321 -

[911] She who is as pretty as the moon – Glory,
She is peace in the heart of the devotee,
[912] She who is consort of Sada Shiv – Glory,
Her family consists of perpetual glories.
- 322 -

---

[907] तत्वाधिका *Tatwa-adikaa*

[908] तत्वमयी *Tatwa-mayee*

[909] तत्वमर्त्थस्वरूपिणी *Tat-twam-artha-swaroopinee*

[910] सामगानप्रिया *Saama-gaana-priyaa;* * Veda

[911] सौम्या *Soumyaa*

[912] सदाशिवकुटुम्बिनी *Sadaa-shiva-kutumbinee*

Shloka 169.

सव्यापसव्यमार्ग्गस्था सर्व्वापद्विनिवारिणी
स्वस्था स्वभावमधुरा धीरा धीरसमर्च्चिता ॥१६९

Savya-apasavya-maarga-st'thaa Sarva-aapath-vinivaarinee
Swa-st'thaa Swa-bhaava-madhuraa Dheeraa Dheera-sama-arch'chitha
169.

[913]She who the birth, death and living be,
She likes methods tantric and priestly,
[914]She who removes all dangers – Glory,
[915]She is free from all disturbances – Glory.
- 323 -

[916]She is by Her nature sweet – Glory,
[917]She who is courageous – Glory,
[918]She adored for the wise – Glory,
She revered by courageous – Glory.
- 324 -

---

[913] सव्यापसव्यमार्ग्गस्था Savya-apasavya-maarga-st'thaa

[914] सर्व्वापद्विनिवारिणी Sarva-aapath-vinivaarinee

[915] स्वस्था Swa-st'thaa

[916] स्वभावमधुरा Swa-bhaava-madhuraa

[917] धीरा Dheeraa

[918] धीरसमर्च्चिता Dheera-sama-arch'chithaa

श्री ललिता सहस्रनाम

Shloka 170.

चैतन्याघर्यसमाराध्या चैतन्यकुसुमप्रिया
सदोदिता सदातुष्टा तरुणादित्यपाटला ॥१७०

Chaitanya-aarghya-sam-aaraadhyaa Chaithanya-kusuma-priyaa
Sada-o-udithaa Sadaa-thushtaa Tharuna-aadithya-paatalaa
170.

[919]She be worshipped with mind only,
[920]She likes never fading flowers – Glory,
Peaceful, mind-control, giving, kind be,
Knowledge, perseverance, truth – Glory.
- 325 -

[921]She who is always illuminant – Glory,
She illuminates the heart of the saintly,
[922]She who is always satisfied – Glory,
[923]She is beauty of the rising sun – Glory.
- 326 -

---

[919] चैतन्याघर्यसमाराध्या *Chaitanya-aarghya-sam-aaraadhyaa*
[920] चैतन्यकुसुमप्रिया *Chaithanya-kusuma-priyaa*
[921] सदोदिता *Sada-o-udithaa*
[922] सदातुष्टा *Sadaa-thushtaa*
[923] तरुणादित्यपाटला *Tharuna-aadithya-paatalaa*

Shloka 171.

दक्षिणादक्षिणाराध्या दरस्मेरमुखांबुजा
कालिनीकेवलाऽनर्घ्यकैवल्यपददायिनी ॥१७१

Dakshina-adakshina-aaradhyaa Dara-smaera-mukha-ambujaa
Kaalinee Kaevalaa-anarghya-kaivalya-pada-daayinee

171.

[924]She loved by learned and ignorant – Glory,
[925]Her smiling face, lotus in bloom be – Glory,
[926]She is beyond measurable time – Glory,
[927]She gives infinite heavenly stature – Glory.

- 327 -

Shloka 172.

स्तोत्रप्रिया स्तुतिमती श्रुतिसंस्तुतवैभवा
मनस्विनी मानवती महेशी मंगलाकृति: ॥१७२

Sthoethra-priyaa Sthuthi-matheee Shruthi-sam-sthutha-vaibhavaa
Manaswinee Manavathee Maha-esee Managala-akr'thih

172.

[928]She fond of hymns in praise – Glory,
She who enjoys Her chants – Glory,
[929] She rewards who sing her chants truly,
[930]She worshipped by the Vedas – Glory.

- 328 -

---

[924] दक्षिणादक्षिणाराध्या Dakshina-adakshina-aaradhyaa
[925] दरस्मेरमुखांबुजा Dara-smaera-mukha-ambujaa
[926] कालिनीकेवला Kaalinee kaevalaa
[927] अनर्घ्यकैवल्यपददायिनी Anarghya-kaivalya-pada-daayinee
[928] स्तोत्रप्रिया Sthoethra-priyaa
[929] स्तुतिमती Sthuthi-matheee
[930] श्रुतिसंस्तुतवैभवा Shruthi-sam-sthutha-vaibhavaa

श्री ललिता सहस्रनाम

[931] She who has a stable mind – Glory,
[932] She who has a big heart – Glory,
[933] She the greatest goddess – Glory,
[934] She who does only good – Glory.

- 329 -

Shloka 173.

विश्वमाता जगद्धात्री विशालाक्षी विरागि--णी

प्रगल्भा परमोदारा परामोदा मनोमयी ॥१७३

Vishwa-maathaa Jagath-dhaathree Vishaala-akshee Vi-raaginee
Pragalbhaa Param-o-udaara Para-aamoedaa Mana-o-mayee

173.

[935] She mother of universe – Glory,
[936] She supports the world – Glory,
[937] She sees everything – Glory,
[938] She without attachments – Glory,

- 330 -

[939] She who is courageous – Glory,
[940] She who is the great giver – Glory,
[941] She has great happiness – Glory,
[942] She who is one with mind – Glory.

- 331 -

---

[931] *मनस्विनी Manaswinee*

[932] *मानवती Maanavathee*

[933] *महेशी Maha-esee*

[934] *मंगलाकृतिः Managala-akr'thee*

[935] *विश्वमाता Vishwa-maatha*

[936] *जगद्धात्री Jagath-dhaathree*

[937] *विशालाक्षी Vishaala-akshee*

[938] *विरागि--णी Vi-raaginee*

[939] *प्रगल्भा Pragalbhaa*

[940] *परमोदारा Param-o-udaara*

[941] *परामोदा Para-aamoedaa*

[942] *मनोमयी Mana-o-mayee*

Shloka 174.

व्योमकेशी विमानस्था वज्रिणी वामकेश्वरी
पञ्चयज्ञप्रिया पञ्चप्रेतमञ्चाधिशायिनी ॥१७४

Vyoma-kaesee Vimaana-st'thaa Vajrinee Vaamaka-eswaree
Pancha-yajna-priyaa Pancha-praeta-mancha-adi-shaayinee

174.

[943]She the universe, Her hair sky be,
[944] She who is at the very top – Glory,
[945]She adorned with diamonds be,
A part of Her is Indra's wife – Glory.
- 332 -

[946]She idol who follow left path – Glory,
[947]She likes five offerings from devotee,
[948]She sleeps on five corpses – Glory,
She be with devotee after death – Glory.
- 333 -

[943] व्योमकेशी Vyoma-kaesee
[944] विमानस्था Vimaana-st'thaa
[945] वज्रिणी Vajrinee
[946] वामकेश्वरी Vaamaka-eswaree
[947] पञ्चयज्ञप्रिया Pancha-yajna-priyaa
[948] पञ्चप्रेतमञ्चाधिशायिनी Pancha-praeta-mancha-adi-shaayinee

श्री ललिता सहस्रनाम

Shloka 175.

पञ्चमी पञ्चभूतेशी पञ्चसंख्योपचारिणी
शाश्वती शाश्वतैश्वर्य्या शर्म्मदा शंभुमोहिनी ॥१७५

Panchameee Pancha-bhootha-esee Pancha-sankhya-o-upa-chaarinee
Shaashwathee Shaashwatha-aishwaryaa Sharma-daa Shambhu-moehinee
175.

[949] She consort of Lord SadShiv* – Glory,
[950] She chief of Pancha bhoothas* – Glory,
[951] She worshipped in five ways* – Glory,
[952] She who is clearly permanent – Glory.
- 334 -

[953]She who gives perennial wealth – Glory,
[954]She who gives total pleasure – Glory,
[955]She is and creates the desire – Glory,
She who bewitches Lord Shiv – Glory.
- 335 -

---

[949] पञ्चमी Panchameee; * fifth of the pancha brahmas

[950] पञ्चभूतेशी Pancha-bhootha-esee; * earth, sky, fire, air and water

[951] पञ्चसंख्योपचारिणी Pancha-sankhya-o-upa-chaarinee; * Gandha (sandal wood),
Pushpa (flower), Dhoopa (incense), dheepa (light), Naivedya (offering)

[952] शाश्वती Shaashwathee

[953] शाश्वतैश्वर्य्या Shaashwatha-aishwaryaa

[954] शर्म्मदा Sharma-daa

[955] शंभुमोहिनी Shambhu-moehinee

Shloka 176.

धरा धरसुता धन्या धर्मिणी धर्म्मवर्द्धिनी
लोकातीता गुणातीता सर्व्वातीता शमात्मिका ॥१७६

Dharaa Dhara-suthaa Dhanyaa Dharminee Dharma-varddhinee
Loeka-atheethaa Guna-atheethaa Sarva-atheethaa Shama-aathmikaa

176.

[956]She supports everything – Glory,
[957]She is Parvathi and Sita – all Glory,
She daughter of mountain – Glory,
[958]She worthy to meditate on – Glory.
- 336 -

She the source of all wealth – Glory,
[959]She who is ever righteous – Glory,
[960]She surges righteousness – Glory,
She makes dharma grow – Glory.
- 337 -

[961]She is beyond the world – Glory,
[962]She beyond three natural qualities*,
[963] She is beyond everything – Glory,
[964] She is but eternal peace – Glory.
- 338 -

---

[956] धरा *Dharaa*

[957] धरसुता *Dhara-suthaa*

[958] धन्या *Dhanyaa*

[959] धर्मिणी *Dharminee*

[960] धर्म्मवर्द्धिनी *Dharma-vardhinee*

[961] लोकातीता *Loeka-atheethaa*

[962] गुणातीता *Guna-atheetha; * of satwa, rajas and tama*

[963] सर्व्वातीता *Sarva-atheethaa*

[964] शमात्मिका *Shama-aathmikaa*

Shloka 177.

बन्धूककुसुमप्रख्या बाला लीलाविनोदिनी
सुमंगली सुखकरी सुवेषाढ्या सुवासिनी ॥१७७

Bandhooka-kusuma-prakhyaa Baalaa Leela-vinodinee
Su-mangalee Sukha-karee Su-vaesha-aadhya Su-vaasinee
177.

[965]She glows as bhandhook flower truly,
[966]She who is a young maiden – Glory,
She who is of perpetual youth – Glory,
[967]She plays creation, destruction – Glory.
- 339 -

[968]She who gives all good things – Glory,
[969]She who gives real pleasure – Glory,
[970] She who is well made up – Glory,
[971]She manifests as fragrance – Glory.
- 340 -

---

[965] बन्धूककुसुमप्रख्या *Bandhooka-kusuma-prakhyaa*

[966] बाला *Baalaa*

[967] लीलाविनोदिनी *Leela-vinodinee*

[968] सुमंगली *Su-mangalee*

[969] सुखकरी *Sukha-karee*

[970] सुवेषाढ्या *Su-vaesha-aadhya*

[971] सुवासिनी *Su-vaasinee*

Shloka 178.

सुवासिन्यच्चर्चनप्रीताऽऽशोभना शुद्धमानसा
बिन्दुतर्प्पणसन्तुष्टा पूर्व्वजा त्रिपुरांबिका ॥१७८

Su-vasini-arch'chana-preeta-aashobhanaa Shudha-maansaa
Bindu-tharppana-santhushtaa Poorva-jaa Thri-pura-ambikaa

178.

[972]She likes married lady's worship – Glory,
[973]She ever glows with illuminance – Glory,
[974]She who with the pure mind – Glory,
She in the heart of the saintly – Glory.
- 341 -

She who has a clean mind – Glory,
[975]She fond of worship by saintly – Glory,
[976] She who preceded everyone – Glory,
[977]She mother to three states – Glory.
- 342 -

---

[972] सुवासिन्यच्चर्चनप्रीता *Su-vasini-arch'chana-preethaa*

[973] आशोभना *Aa-shobhanaa*

[974] शुद्धमानसा *Shudha-maansaa*

[975] बिन्दुतर्प्पणसन्तुष्टा *Bindu-tharppana-santhushtaa*

[976] पूर्व्वजा *Poorva-jaa*

[977] त्रिपुरांबिका *Thri-pura-ambikaa; * of awakening, dream and sleep*

Shloka 179.

दशमुद्रासमाराध्या त्रिपुराश्रीवशंकरी

ज्ञानमुद्रा ज्ञानगम्या ज्ञानज्ञेयस्वरूपिणी ॥१७९

Dasa-mudraa-sam-aaradhyaa Thri-pura-shree-vasham-karee
Jnaana-mudra Jnaana-gamyaa Jnaana-jneya-swa-roopinee
                                                            179.

[978]She revered by all symbols – Glory,
[979]She fourth state of consciousness* be,
[980]She denoted, [981]reached by wise only,
[982]She known through wisdom* – Glory.
- 343 -

Shloka 180.

योनिमुद्रा त्रिखण्डेशी त्रिगुणाऽम्बा त्रिकोणगा

अनघाऽद्भुतचारित्रा वाञ्चितार्थप्रदायिनी ॥१८०

Yoeni-mudraa Tri-khanda-esee Thri-guna-ambaa Thri-kona-gaa
Anaghaa Athbhutha-chaarithraa Vaanchitha-art'tha-pradaayinee
                                                            180.

[983]She symbol, source of universe be,
[984]She the lord of three zones – Glory,
[985]She on whom the three qualities be,
[986]She the mother of whole universe be.
- 344 -

---

[978] *दशमुद्रासमाराध्या Dasa-mudraa-sam-aaradhyaa*

[979] *त्रिपुराश्रीवशंकरी Thri-pura-shree-vasham-karee; * beyond awakening, dream and sleep*

[980] *ज्ञानमुद्रा Jnaana-mudra*

[981] *ज्ञानगम्या Jnaana-gamyaa*

[982] *ज्ञानज्ञेयस्वरूपिणी Jnaana-jneya-swa-roopinee; awareness of the inner self*

[983] *योनिमुद्रा Yoeni-mudraa*

[984] *त्रिखण्डेशी Tri-khanda-esee; * of fire, moon and sun*

[985] *त्रिगुणा Thri-gunaa*

[986] *अंबा Ambaa*

987 She got at vertices of triangle – Glory,
988 She who is not neared by sin – Glory,
989 She has a wonderful history – Glory,
990 She gives what is desired – Glory.
- 345 -

Shloka 181.

अभ्यासातिशयज्ञाता षडद्ध्वातीतरूपिणी

अव्याजकरुणामूर्त्तिः अज्ञानध्वान्तदीपिका ॥१८१

Abhyaasaa-athishaya-jnaathaa Shada-adhwa-athetha-roopinee
Avyaaja-karuna-moorthih ajnaana-dwaantha-deepika

181.

991 She realized by constant practice – Glory,
992 She beyond knowledge does be – Glory,
993 She shows mercy without reason – Glory,
994 She the lamp that rids ignorance – Glory.
- 346 -

---

987 त्रिकोणगा Thri-kona-gaa

988 अनघा Anaghaa

989 अद्भुतचारित्रा Athbhutha-chaarithraa

990 त्र्थप्रदायिनी Vaanchitha-art'tha-pradaayinee

991 अभ्यासातिशयज्ञाता Abhyaasaa-athishaya-jnaathaa

992 षडद्ध्वातीतरूपिणी Shada-adhwa-atheetha-roopinee

993 अव्याजकरुणामूर्त्तिः Avyaaja-karuna-moorthi

994 अज्ञानध्वान्तदीपिका Ajnaana-dwaantha-deepika

Shloka 182.

आबालगोपविदिता सर्वानुल्लंघ्यशासना

श्रीचक्रराजनिलया श्रीमद्त्रिपुरसुन्दरी ॥१८२

Aabaala-goepa-vidithaa Sarvaan-ullanghya-shaasanaa
Sree-chakra-raaja-nilayaa Sree-mat-thri-pura-sundaree

182.

[995] She who is worshipped by all – Glory,
[996] Her orders never be disobeyed – Glory,
[997] She is the core of everything – Glory,
[998] Great beauty in three states* – Glory.
- 347 -

Shloka 183.

श्रीशिवा शिवशक्त्यैक्यरूपिणी ललितांबिका

एवं श्रीललिता देव्याः नाम नाम सहस्रकम जगुह ॥१८३

Shree-shivaa Shiva-shakti-aikya-roopinee Laita-ambikaa
Evam shri lalitadevya nam nam sahasrakam jaguh

183.

[999] She who is the eternal peace – Glory,
She creates, keeps, dissolves all – Glory,
[1000] She union of Shiv and Shakti – Glory,
[1001] She easily approachable mother – Glory.
- 348 -

ॐ श्रीललितांबिकायै नमः

---

[995] आबालगोपविदिता

[996] सर्वानुल्लंघ्यशासना *Sarvaan-ullanghya-shaasanaa*

[997] श्रीचक्रराजनिलया *Sree-chakra-raaja-nilayaa*

[998] श्रीमद्त्रिपुरसुंदरी *Sree-mat-thri-pura-sundaree; * life of awareness, dream and sleep*

[999] श्रीशिवा *Shree-shivaa*

[1000] शिवशक्त्यैक्यरूपिणी *Shiva-shakti-aikya-roopinee*

[1001] ललितांबिका *Lalitha-ambikaa*

Phala Sruthi

As in Devi Bhagavatham and Devi Puranam be,
Benefits[1002] of chanting Laita Sahasranama be;

And Phala sruthi the next chapter herein does be,
It is not recited with Laitha Sahasranama plainly.

Nama sahasram khaditham they ghatothbhava,
Rahasyaanam rahasyam cha Laita preethi dayakam,
Aanena sadrusam stotram na bhootham na bhavishyathi.

1.

Oh Agastya! These 1000 names told but be,
Secret of the secrets - very dear to Laita Devi;

This type of prayer has never existed previously,
And will never be present in the future definitely.
- 1 -

Sarva roga prasamanam sarva sampath pravardhanam,
Sarvaapath mruthyu shamanam akala mruthyu nivaranam.

2.

It cures all diseases, gives rise to wealth fully,
Rids accidental deaths, antidote to death untimely;
- 2 -

Sarva jwararthi hananam deergayushya pradhayakam,
Puthra pradhama puthraanaam purushartha pradhayakam.

3.

It cures fever and gives rise to long life clearly,
It blesses with first son, gives three wealths truly;
- 3 -

Yidham visesharidevya sthothram preethi vidhatakam,
Japen nityam prayathnena lalithopasthi thath para.

4.

This special prayer of goddess pleases Laita Devi,
Should be chanted after worshipping of Laita daily;
- 4 -

[1002] *materialistic and Spiritual*

Pratha snathwa vidhathena sandhya karma samapya cha,
Pooja gruhe thatho gathwa chakra rajam samarchayeth

5.

Take bath in morning, finish oblations of dawn early,
Go to prayer room, first worship Sree Chakra truly;
- 5 -

Vidhyam japeth sahasram vaa trishtatha shathameva cha,
Rahasya naama saahasra midham paschad paden nara.

6.

Chant Sri Vidya mantra 100 or 400 times reverently,
Then these secret thousand names should read be.
- 6 -

Janama madhye sakruchapi ya yevam padathe sudhee,
Thasya punya phalam vakshye srunu thwam Kumbha Sambhava.

7.

Sage born out of the pot, please hear result clearly,
Of reading these in the middle of life by devotees;
- 7 -

Gangadhi sarva theertheshu ya snayath koti janmasu,
Koti linga prathishtam thu ya kuryadh vimukthake.

8.

Kurukshethre thu yo dadyath koti vaaram ravi gruhe,
Koti sournabharanam srothreeyeshu dwijanmasu

9.

Ya kotim hayamedhanaa maharedh gaangarodhasee,
Achareth koopa kotiyom nirjare maru bhoothale.

10.

Durbhikshe ya prathi dhinam koti brahmana bhojanam,
Sradhaya parayaa kuryath sahasra parivathsaraan.

11.

Effected by bathing in rivers as Ganga devotee be,
Or a crore times same effect as a crore lingas holy;
- 8 -

Or a crore times in Kurukshetra on Sunday giving be,
A crore gold ornaments to twice born Veda knowing be;
- 9 -

Or doing a crore Aswa-medha yagas on Ganges keenly,
Or digging one crore water-wells in deserts honestly;
- 10 -

Or feeding a crore Brahmins during the famine daily,
Or training/teaching one thousand children sincerely;.
- 11 -

Thath punyam koti gunitham labhyeth punyamanuthamam,
Rahasya nama saahasre namno apyekasya keerthanaath,

12.

A crore times good effect of all these blessings be,
By chanting a name of a thousand secret names truly;
- 12 -

Rahasya nama saahasre namaikaapi ya padeth,
Thasya paapani nasyanthi mahanthyaapi na samsaya.

13.

If a name among thousand secret names read be,
All sins committed, destroyed without doubt do be;
- 13 -

Nithya karmanushtaana nishidhakaranadhapi,
Yath paapam jayathe pumsam thath sarva nasyathi drutham.

14.

Sin by bad act of not doing sacred routines daily,
Would go away, all sins are destroyed speedily;
- 14 -

Bahunathra kimukthena srunu thwam kalasi sutha,
Aathraika namne yaa Shakti pathakaanaam nivarthathe,
Thannivarthya magham karthum naalam loka schadurdasa.

15.

Sage Agastya!, Hear how most people get free,
By chanting for getting rid of sins to their ability;
For these, without any doubt would remove fully,
All sins committed in fourteen lokas undoubtedly;
- 15 -

Yasthyakthwa nama sahasaram papa hani mabhhepsathi,
Sa hi seethe nivrthyartha hima shailam nishevathe.

16.

Who want to rid sins yet hate to chant faithfully,
It like going to Himalayas to get rid of cold be;
- 16 -

Bhaktho ya keerthyen nithya midham nama sahasrakam,
Thasmai sri Laita devi preethabheeshtam prayachathi.

17.

Devotees who sing these thousand names daily,
By fulfilling their wishes be blessed by Laita Devi;
- 17 -

Akeerthayennidham sthothram kadham bhaktho bhavishyathi.

18.

How can he who does not sing them be a devotee?
- 18 -

Nithyam keerthanashaktha keerthayeth punya vasare,
Samkrathou vishuve chaiva swajanma thrithayeyane.

19.

Who sing it not daily, on occasions chant actually,
As first of every month, new year, birthdays[1003] truly;
- 19 -

Navamyaam vaa chathurdasyam sithaayaam shukravasare,
Keerthyen nama sahasram pournamasyaam viseshatha.

20.

On Navami or Chathurdasi or Fridays sincerely,
And on full moon day singing this very special be;
- 20 -

Pournamasyam chandra Bhimbhe dhyathwa sri Laitaambikaam,
Panchopacharai sampoojya paden nama sahasrakam.

21.

Sarva roga pranasyanthi deergamayuscha vindhathi,
Ayam aayushkaro nama prayoga kalpanoditha,

22.

On full moon day facing full moon, meditating on Devi,
Offer five oblations and by reading thousand names truly;
- 21 -

All diseases will vanish, long life would given be,
Accompany with Aayushkara prayoga[1004] justly;
- 22 -

[1003] *Self, wife and son*
[1004] *rite to get long life*

Jwarartha shiirasimsprushtwa paden nama sahasrakam,
Thath kshnaath yaathi shiraamsthadho jwaropi cha.

23.

If with fever, touches his head, chants devotedly,
Fever descends from the head and vanish slowly;
- 23 -

Sarva vyadhi nivruthyartha sprushtwa bhasma japedhidham,
Thad bhasma dharanadeva nasyanthi vyadhaya kshanaath.

24.

For ridding diseases chant it and touch ash holy,
By wearing that ash all diseases be cured directly;
- 24 -

Jalam samanthrasya kumbhastham nama sahasratho mune,
Aabhishichedha graham grasthaan graham nasyanthi thath kshanaath.

25.

Storing water in pot, and chanting it sincerely,
On anointing self with that water, rids problems[1005] fully;
- 25 -

Sudha sagara madhyastham dhyathwa Sri Laitambikaam,
Ya paden nama sahasram visham thasya vinasyathi.

26.

Meditating on Goddess Laitambika and Lakshmi,
If thousand names are read, poison effect washed be;
- 26 -

Vandhyaanaam puthralabhaaya, nama saahasra manthridham,
Navaneetham pradadyathu, puthralabho bhaved druvam.

27.

For a son chant these thousand names devotedly,
Offer butter to God - she will blessed with a son be;
- 27 -

Rajakarshana kaamasche drajavasadha ding mukha,

28.

Trirathram cha padeth ethad, sridevi dhyana thathpara,
Sa raja paravasyena thurangam vaa matham gajam.

29.

[1005] *created by planets - Graha Doshas , Sade Sathi , Shani Dosha , Kala Sarpa dosha*
etc.

Aarohya yathi nikatam dasavath prani pathya cha,
Thasmai rajyam cha kosam dadhya deva vasangatha.

30.

For attracting or facing people with authority,

Read the thousand names of Goddess sincerely;
- 28 -

Then person with authority under your control be,

Would ride a horse or elephant unquestionably;
- 29 -

Come to your side, would salute and serve truly,

Offer you his country or a state of his country.[1006]
- 30 -

Rahasya nama sahasram ya keerthyathi nithyasa,
Than mukhaloka mathrena muhye loka thrayam mune.

31.

As soon as they see the face of who chants truly,

Thousand secret names daily, saints salute surely;
- 31 -

Yasthvidham nama sahasram sakruth padathi bhakthiman,
Thasya yea sasthravasthesham nihantha Sharabheswara.

32.

Who reads these thousand names – his enemies,

Will be killed by arrows of Sharabheswar[1007] certainly;
- 32 -

Yo vabhicharam kuruthe nama sahasra padake,
Nivarthya thath kriyaam hanyatham vai prathyangira swayam.

33.

[1006] *Your words/requests will not be turned down by any one – even by people of influence or those who are in powerful positions in society.*
[1007] *Your dis-tractors/enemies will not succeed against you*

Who does black magic on Devi's names reader be,
Killed by Prathyangira devi[1008] who protects devotee.
- 33 -

Yea Kroora drushtya veekshanthe nama sahasra padakam,
Thaan andhaan kuruthe ksipram swayam marthanda bhirava.

34.

He who sees reader of thousand names with cruelty,
Is blinded by Marthanda Bhairav[1009] himself immediately;
- 34 -

Dhanam yo harathe chorair nama sahasra japeen,
Yathra kuthra sthiram vaapi Kshethra palo nihanthi thaam.

35.

He who steals wealth of reader of thousand names be,
Killed wherever he hides by The Kshethra pala finally;
- 35 -

Vidhyasu kuruthe vadham yo vidwan nama jaapeena,
Thasya vak sthambhanam sadhya karothi Nakuleshwari.

36.

Who argues with wise who reads thousand names daily,

Would be made dumb by Nakuleshwari immediately[1010];
- 36 -

Yo raja kuruthe vairam nama sahasra japeen,
Chathuranga balam thasya Dandinee samhareth swayam.

37.

King's army who attacks thousand names reader be,

An enemy destroyed by Dandinee herself immediately;
- 37 -

Ya paden nama saahasram shan masam bhakthi samyutha,
Lakshmi chanchalya rahitha sada thishtathi thad gruhe.

38.

[1008] *Most fierce and powerful avatar of Devi*
[1009] *Those who plan ill deeds against the one who chants this will be distracted or blinded by other thoughts that he will not be able to execute his plans*
[1010] *Nobody can win argument against the devotee who chants the Lalitha Sahasranama*

Who reads the thousand names six months devotedly,

Has fickle minded Wealth Goddess at home lastingly.
- 38 -

Masamekam prathi dhinam, thri vaaram ya paden nara,
Bharathi thasya jihvagre range nruthyathi nithyasa.

39.

Who reads it for a month or at least three weeks daily,

Has Saraswati, Wisdom Goddess on his tongue surely;
- 39 -

Ya paden nama saaharam janma madhye sakrunnera,
Thad drushi gochara sarve muchyathi sarva kilbihai.

40.

Who reads the thousand names in middle-life truly,
Sees everything and all his sins would pardoned be;
- 40 -

Yo vethi naama sahaasram thasmai dheyam dwijanmane,
Annam vasthram dhanam dhanyam nanyebhyasthu kada chana.

41.

Who makes thousand names his - twice born will surely,
Get food, cloths, wealth, cereals, all he wishes definitely;
- 41 -

Sri manthra rajam yo vethi sri chakram ya samarchathi,
Ya keerthayathi naamaani tham sath pathram vidhur budha,

42.

Who learns Sri Mantras King, offers Sri Chakram loyally,
Sings these thousand names, be deemed by learned holy;
- 42 -

Thasmai dheyam prayathnena Sri Devi preethimichata,
Ya keerthayathi namaani manthra rajam na vethi ya.

43.

To him goddess gives with love, what he wants surely,
Who sings these names, learns king of Mantras totally;
- 43 -

Pasu thulya sa vijneya thasmai datham nirarthakam,
Pareekshya vidhya vidhusha thasmai dadhya dwichakshana.

44.

No point in giving this Mantra to who animal like be,
It should be given to those who learned and wise be;
- 44 -

Sri manthra raja sadruso yadha manthro na vidhyathe,
Devatha Laita thulyaa yadhaa nasthi ghatodhbhava.

45.

There no chants which equal to Sri Mantra Raja be,
Agastya! There no goddess equivalent to Lalita be,
- 45 -

Rahasya nama saahasra thulyaa nasthi thadha sthuthi,
Likhithwa pusthake yasthu nama saahasram uthamam .

46.

Samarchayed sada bhakthya thasya thushyathi Sundari,
Bahunathra kimukthena srunu thwam Kumbha sambhava.

47.

There no prayer greater than secret thousand names be,
And he who writes it in a book, the thousand names truly;
- 46 -

And submits to her, would make the pretty one happy,
Please hear much more about it, Sage Agastya openly;
- 47 -

Naanena sadrusam stotram sarva thanthreshu vidhyathe,
Thasmad upasako nithyam keerthyedhida madarath,

48.

There no prayer any where in literature of Tantra does be,
So those who practice Tantra sing it with devotion daily;
- 48 -

Yebhir nama sahasthraishtu Sri Chakram yo aarchayedh sakruth,
Padmair va thulasee pushpai, kalhaarai vaa, kadambakai.

49.

Champakair jathee mallika kara veerakai.
Uthpalai bilwa pathrer vaa, kunda kesara patalai.

50.

श्री ललिता सहस्रनाम

Aanyai sugandhi kusumai kethaki madhavee mukhai,
Thasya punya phalm vakthum na saknothi Mahesvara.

51.

Even Lord Shiv would not be able to tell adequately,
Effect of adoring Sri Chakra by thousand names fully;
- 49 -

With lotus, Kalharra, kadamba flowers, leaves of tulsi,
Jasmine, Champak, Kara veera, Utpal leaves of Bilwa surely;
- 50 -

Jasmine buds and Kesara flowers ever offered reverently,
And scented flowers like lots, Kethaki Madave Mukha truly;
- 51 -

Sa vethi Laita devi saw chakrarchanajam phalam,
Aanye kadham vijaaneeyur Brahmadhyaa swalpa medhasa.

52.

Only Laita can tell result of worshipping her chakra clearly,
And Lord Brahma may narrate it to certain extent possibly;
- 52 -

Prathi masam pournamasya mabhir nama sahasrakai,
Rathrou yas chakra rajastha marchayeth para devathaam,

53.

Sa yeva Laita roopa sthad roopa Laita swayam,
Na thayo vidhyathe bhedho bedha ckruth papakruth bhavedh.

54.

In every month during full moon day, if she worshipped be,
By the thousand names, in night on Sri Chakra devotedly;
- 53 -

He would himself have form of goddess Laita Devi,
He not seen as another - for that would but a sin be;
- 54 -

Maha navamyam yo bhaktha Sri Devi chakra madhyagaam,
Archaye nnama saahasrai sthasya mukthi kare sthithaa.

55.

The devotee who worships her on mahanavami actually,
On Sri Chakra the thousand names attains salvation truly;
- 55 -

Yasthu nama sahasrena Shukra vare samarchayeth,
Chakra rajo maha devim thasya punya phalam srunu.

56.

If these thousand names dedicated on Friday do be,
To Sri Chakra of the goddess - hear benefits clearly;
- 56 -

Sarvan kaamaan vpyeha, sarva soubhagya samyutha,
Puthra pouthradhi samyuktho bhukthwa bhogaan yadepsithaan.

57.

All your desires be fulfilled and life blessed will be,
Enjoying all pleasures, surrounded by sons, progeny;
- 57 -

Aanthe Laita devya sayujyam adhi durlabham,
Prathaneeyam shivadhyaischa prapnothyeva na samsaya,

58.

At end bget salvation under Laita, which difficult be,
Get all benefits of praying to Gods like Shiv certainly;
- 58 -

Ya sahasram Brahmanaana mebhir nama sahasrakai,
Samarchaya bhojayedh bhakthya payasa poopa shad rasai.

59.

Thadsmai preenaathi Laita swasamrajyam prayachathi.
Na thasya durlabham vasthu thrishulokeshu vidhyathe.

60.

Dedicating these thousand names to thousand Brahmins be,
Feeding them with sweet Payasam, Vada of black gram truly;

And a meal which is blessed with all six tastes completely,
Would make one dear to the Goddess Laita Devi definitely;
- 59 -

And she would bless you with her kingdom and bliss fully,
There nothing in the three worlds would unachievable be;
- 60 -

Nishkama keerthayedhyasthu nama Sahasramuthamam,
Brahma jnana mavapnothi yena muchyathe bandanath.

61.

Who chants these names without desire, attachment truly,

Begets wisdom of Brahman - freed from life bonds be;
- 61 -

Dhanarthi dhanam aapnothi, Yasorthi prapnuyath yasa,
Vidhyarthi cha aapnuyath vidhya, nama sahasra keerthanaath.

62.

One who wants money, fame or knowledge will certainly,

By singing these thousand names achieve desire surely;
- 62 -

Naanena sadhrusham sthothram Bhoga moksha pradham mune,
Keethaneeyamidham thasmad bhoga mokshadhibhir narai,

63.

No prayer like this gives pleasures and salvation actually,

By singing thousand names pleasure, salvation got truly;
- 63 -

Chathurashrama nishtaicha keerthaneeyamidham sada,
Swadharma samanushtaana vaikalya paripoorthaye.

64.

In all stages[1011] of life singing these names devotedly,

And with Dharma helps reach goal without difficulty.
- 64 -

Kalou papaika bahule dharmanushtana varjathe,
Namanu keerthanam mukthwa nrunaam nanya paraayanam.

65.

In the age of Kali[1012], when all Dharmas forsaken do be,
Men would get salvation by singing these names only.
- 65 -

[1011] *4 Stages – Baalyam , Youvanam , Grahasthashramam , Vanaprastham , Sanyasam*
[1012] *This Yuga – Kali Yuga*

Loukeekath vachanath mukhyam Vishnu nama keerthanam,
Vishnu nama saharaischa Shiv namaikamuthamam.

66.

In family life it is important to sing Vishnu's name surely,
But better than that is singing names of Lord Shiv clearly.
- 66 -

Shiv nama sahasraischa devyaa namaikamuthamam,
Devi Nama sahasraani kotisa santhi Kumbhaja.

67.

Better than thousand names of Shiv, names of Devi be,
Agastya! Devi's Thousand names a crore times better be;
- 67 -

Theshu mukhyam dasa vidham nama sahasra muchyathe,
Rahasyanama saahasramidham sashtham dasaswapi.

68.

There ten[1013] important names of these thousand names be,
And all these important names are ever praise and worthy;
- 68 -

Thasmad sankeethayennithyam kali dosha nivruthaye,
Mukhyam Sri mathu naamethi na janathi vimohithaa.

69.

Singing them daily would cure the ill effects of age Kali,
The name Mata is important and should not forgotten be;
- 69 -

Vishnu nama paraa kechith Shiv nama paraa pare,
Na kaschid aapi lokeshu Laita nama thathpara.

70.

Better than names of Vishnu the names of Shiv be,
But in all worlds nothing better than names of Laita be;
- 70 -

Yenanya devathaa nama keerthitham Janama kotishu,
Thasyaiva bhavathi sradhaa Sri devi nama keerthane.

71.

[1013] *Ganga, Gayathri, Syamala, Lakshmi, Kali, Bala, Laita, Rajarajeswari, Saraswathi and Bhavani*

श्री ललिता सहस्रनाम

If names of other Gods sung in crores of births be,

It is equal to singing the thousand names devotedly;
- 71 -

Charame janmani yadha Sri vidhyaupasako bhaveth,
Nama sahasra padascha thadha charama janmani.

72.

If you at your last birth an Upasaka of Sri Vidhya be,

By reading the thousand names, this your last birth be;
- 72 -

Yadhaiva virala loke sri vidyachara vedhina,
Thadaiva viralo guhya nama saahasthra pataka.

73.

In this world to find Upasakas of Sri Vidhya it rare be,

Also rare to find who read these thousand names truly;
- 73 -

Manthra raja japaschaiva chakra rajarchanam thadha,
Rahasya nama patascha naalpayasya thapas phalam.

74.

Chanting king of chants followed by Sri Chakra be,

Reading the thousand names - same as Austerity[1014];
- 74 -

Apadannama saahasram preenayedhyaa Maheswareem,
Sa chakshushaa bina roopam pasyedheva vimoodadhi.

75.

Without reading these thousand names or pleasing Devi,
Is like a fool trying to see without the eyes foolishly;
- 75 -

Rahasya nama saahasram thyakthwaa ya sidhi kaamuka,
Sa BHojanam vinaa noonam Kshunnivarthi mabheepsathi.

76.

Forsaking the thousand names, trying occult powers be,
Like satiating hunger after forsaking all meals completely;
- 76 -

[1014] *Thapas*

Yo Bhakthaa Laita devya sa nithyam Keertheyadhidham,
Nanyadhaa preeyathe Devi kalpa koti shathair api.

77.

That devotee who sings these names of Laita Devi,
Need not sing any other for she will pleased be;
- 77 -

Thasmad rahasya naamani, Sri Mathu prayatha padeth,
Yithi they kaditham Stotram rahasyam, Kumbha sambhava.

78.

These thousand names read for making mother happy,
But sage Agastya! This prayer which I told a secret be;
- 78 -

Na vidhyaavedhinebrooya nnama bhakthaya kadachana.,
Yadhaiva gopyaa Sri Vidhya thadha gopyamidham mune.

79.

Learned in Vedas, if they not recite once these names truly,
O sage! The Sri Vidhya would kept secret from them be;
- 79 -

Pasu thulyeshu na broyajjaneshu sthotramuthamam,
Yo dadhadhi vimoodathma Sri vidhya rahithaya thu.

80.

People who do not tell this prayer like animals but be,
If they give Sri Vidhya to foolish without this prayer sadly;
- 80 -

Thasmai kupyanthi yoginya, sonartha sumahaan smruth,
Rahasya nama saahasran thsmad sangopyedhidham.

81.

Yogis would be angry as this leads to problems surely,
So these thousand names as secret from everyone be;
- 81 -

Swathanthrena mayaa noktham thavapi kalasee bhava,
Laita preranaa deva mayoktham stotramuthamam.

82.

Of Sage Agastya, I'd not tell them to you independently,
But for advice by Goddess Laita to tell you categorically;
- 82 -

Keerthaneeya midham bhakthyaa Kumbhayone nirantharam,
Thena thushtaa Maha devi thavabheeshtam pradasyathi.

83.

Oh sage Agastya! Please recite these very devotedly,
The goddess will be pleased, fulfill your wishes fully;
- 83 -

Sootha Uvacha:
Yithyukthwa Sri Hayagreevo dhyathwa Sri Laitambikaam,
Aananda magna hrudaya sadhya pulakitho bhaved.

84.

Sootha said:
After telling thus, sage Hayagriva meditated on Laita Devi,
Was drowned in happiness and became enraptured wholly;
- 84 -

Ithi Sri Brahmanda purane Uthara Kande,
Sri HayagrrevAgastya samvade,
Sri Laita sahasra nama stotra,
Phala srutheernama uthara Bhaga.

85.

Thus ends effect of reciting Laita Sahasranama surely,
Called portion after which in Brahmand Puran but be,
Which a part of the Utara Kanda be undoubtedly,
Discussed between Hayagriva and Agastya holy.
- 85 -

Published Works of Munindra Misra

1. Pt. Kanhaiya Lal Misra - My Father
2. Eddies of Life - My Poems

On Sanatan Dharma

1. Chants of Hindu Gods & Goddesses in English Rhyme
2. Devi Mahatmayam in English Rhyme
3. Goals of Life
4. Lalita Sahasranama in English Rhyme
5. Lord Shiv & Family in English Rhyme
6. Bhagwat Gita – Its Essence in English Rhyme
7. Mahatma Vidur & Chanakiya Neeti in English Rhyme

Web-links:
1. http://mmisrafan.wordpress.com/
2. http://booksmmisra.blogspot.in/
3. http://klmisra.com
4. http://munindramisra.com

Part IV
Family Life

Days on the Farm

When I was a very small child, my parents lived on the farm now owned by the H.E. Thompson family, about two miles from town on the Kingstree-Andrews highway. After my youthful father's death from appendicitis, Mother rented the farm, and she, with her three little daughters, moved to Kingstree. Mary was older than I, and Eula was younger.

Years later, my husband, John D. Britton, and I bought the interests of my relatives and also some extra land adjoining the farm, making about 1,000 acres, but some of it was "bone," land not much good for anything except to hold the world together.

We built a roomy brick house in a beautiful grove there. It had some of the features of which every housekeeper, including me, has dreamed: a spacious living room with plenty of bookshelves and a wide log-burning fireplace; a dining room big enough for family reunions; plenty of cupboards and closets; and also piazzas where needed. To landscape the grounds, which were already dotted with crabapples, wild azaleas, dogwoods and red buds, John gave me his small bonus check that the government had finally issued to the veterans of the First World War. I had a ball with bulbs, more azaleas, evergreens and other plantings.

As we moved to our dream house from our home on the corner of Live Oak Avenue and Kelley Street in Kingstree, we didn't think that we would ever move back to that too-big house, which wasn't old enough to be interesting but was too old to be convenient. We used to vow that the only way all of it could be heated at one time was to set it afire.

After ten short years, we sold the farm to the Thompsons, who had sold their place in Horry County and wanted to move to Williamsburg County, bringing their farm labor with them. I suppose our ten years on the farm had been too good to last. John was free from the strain of politics after having

The Swanns' tombstone in the Williamsburg Cemetery. *Photograph by Linda Brown.*

The house John and Bessie Britton built, with additions, still stands south of Kingstree. *Photograph by Linda Brown.*

Bessie and John's son Jack Britton, a senior in high school in 1937, relaxes at home. *Photograph courtesy of Williamsburgh Historical Museum.*

Frankie Britton Baker. *Photograph courtesy of Williamsburgh Historical Museum.*

Jack and Gladys Britton. *Photograph courtesy of Williamsburgh Historical Museum.*

served several years as clerk of court and in the South Carolina Senate. As he had had a flair for business ever since he was a boy, he was enjoying being free to devote more time to the real estate and timber business he had established in Kingstree some years earlier. We were comfortable financially, which was quite a change from the first years of our marriage.

By then our children had grown up. Our only daughter, Frankie, had finished at Winthrop College for Women and was married to B.W. Baker, whom everybody called Baker, and was living in nearby Georgetown. Our only son, John D. Jr., whom everybody called Jack, had attended Clemson University and was married to a lovely local girl, Gladys Ashburn, and lived in Kingstree. Her only brother, Fred, who was unmarried, lived with his widowed mother, Mrs. Ethel Hodge Ashburn, in Kingstree. All were congenial, and we had many fine times together, with our house as the gathering spot.

But even then, there were faint shadows of trouble ahead of us. The handwriting on the wall was dim, but it was there. The Second World War had seemed far removed, but its tentacles were creeping out to touch every corner of the country. The government had begun to issue orders to civilians in every walk of life, and nobody was free any more.

Problems on a farm the size of ours began multiplying faster than they could be solved with the labor still available. Deep down, John and I knew that the foundation of our easy existence was beginning to crumble, but neither would put it into words.

Suddenly, the war got rolling in high gear. The best of our able-bodied labor was drafted, and the others went to work for fabulous wages in defense plants, leaving crops to spoil in the fields. Then, almost before we could realize it, Baker was in the army, Jack in the paratroops and Fred in the marines, and all had been shipped overseas.

Material from columns originally published in April 1970.

The War Years

We were agonizing through the Second World War—which was then reaching its peak, though we didn't realize that at the time. Baker was in the army, Jack in the paratroops, and Fred in the marines. All were overseas.

Mail was often weeks late. Casualty lists were growing apace, but at times it was more than a month before the next of kin was notified. Many families in Williamsburg County had already been hit hard. A granite marker which the American Legion Post No. 8, erected on the courthouse square on Main Street in Kingstree, lists fifty-eight men who were killed in World War II, not to mention hundreds of others who were wounded.

There were no TVs, but people listened to radio news as often as they could bear it, afraid to listen and afraid not to, cringing under the impending threat of disaster, waiting helplessly for the next blow to fall.

Before the war, Baker and Frankie had been living in Georgetown, where Baker, who had a flair for merchandising, had two retail stores. He sold the stores when he entered the service, and Frankie came back home.

Jack and Gladys had been living in Kingstree, but when Jack left, Gladys gave up their apartment and moved in with her widowed mother, Mrs. Ethel Hodge Ashburn, with whom Fred had been living before he joined the Marines.

With most able-bodied men in the service or otherwise occupied with the war effort, women in unprecedented numbers entered the business world. Frankie worked for Mr. E.C. Epps, head of the Kingstree Production Credit Association. Gladys worked for Mr. David Cribb, manager of the Government Rationing Office. All civilians had to make written application for permission to buy limited amounts of meat, sugar, coffee, shoes, gasoline and tires. No new cars were available.

The Veterans' Memorial on the grounds of the Williamsburg County Courthouse on the day of its dedication, May 10, 1948. *Photograph courtesy of Williamsburgh Historical Museum.*

I had too much idle time in which to worry about the war. Life had already taught me that a busy mind is the best medicine on earth, so I decided to go to work, too. I applied to the secretary of state for a commission as a notary public and opened an office on the courthouse square, where I'm still holding forth.

Frankie and Gladys, who were devoted to each other, spent much of their leisure time together at our house, as did a number of other girls whose husbands were overseas, all forcing themselves to be cheerful but secretly fearful of the next blow to fall. Then, suddenly, it was our turn. The war was nearing its end, but in its last fury, our little world was blasted apart.

First, we received a telegram from Washington. Staff Sergeant Boyce W. Baker, 116 Regiment, 29th Infantry Division, had been shot through the chest in battle in France and was in critical condition. No other details were given. While Baker was still hospitalized far from home, we got another message from Washington; Lieutenant John D. Britton Jr., 513 Regiment, 17th Airborne Division, had been killed in battle in Germany. No other details were given. Jack had just reached twenty-five. Two hours later we got the news from Washington that Private First Class Fred L. Ashburn of the 4th Marines had been killed in battle on the island of Iwo Jima in the Pacific. No other details were given. Fred had just reached the age of nineteen.

Bessie Swann Britton. *Photograph courtesy of Williamsburgh Historical Museum.*

Much later we learned that Jack had been buried in an American cemetery, of which we had never heard, in Holland, and that Fred had been buried in an American cemetery, of which we had never heard, on Iwo Jima.

Jack was tall and powerfully built. On his last trip home, he was in fine physical condition. One day he was standing framed in the door to my room, laughing about how scared he had been when he had to make his

Fred Ashburn. *Photograph courtesy of Williamsburgh Historical Museum.*

LT. JOHN DANIEL BRITTON, JR.
CO. A 513 PARACHUTE REG.
17TH AIRBORNE DIVISION
MARCH 23   MARCH 24
1920   1945
KILLED IN BATTLE AT WESSEL, GERMANY
BURIED AT MARGRATEN, HOLLAND
INTERRED HERE NOV. 7, 1948

Jack Britton's tombstone in the Williamsburg Cemetery. *Photograph by Linda Brown.*

first practice jump from a plane and was certain the parachute would not open in time. I thought then that he looked like a good health poster, with his smiling brown eyes and thick, wavy hair. He used to wish he could swap those waves with his sister for her straight hair.

Life had been unusually good to Jack, and he realized it. He had told me so in occasional serious moments. He had been born with a sense of humor and merry ways, and his hearty laugh was so contagious that others barely in hearing distance had to laugh, too.

I'll always be grateful to J. Dessie O'Bryan Jr., who had been Jack's friend in Kingstree and was then overseas. As soon as he could, he took flowers to Jack's grave, as was the custom at home. The pictures Dessie sent to me were so clear that I could read Jack's name and serial number on the white cross marking his grave among the hundreds of other white crosses standing row on row in the well-kept American Cemetery at Margraten, Holland.

Sometime later, both Jack's and Fred's remains were disinterred and shipped back in flag-draped caskets. At long last, our boys had come home. They were laid to rest beside their ancestors in plots in the Williamsburg Cemetery in Kingstree. Both boys would have wished it so.

Material from columns originally published in April 1970

A Very Present Comfort

The War Department had notified us that Baker had been shot through the chest in battle in France. Jack had been killed in battle in Germany and Fred had been killed in battle on Iwo Jima. Baker had to spend many weary months in Army hospitals before he—mercifully—recovered from his wounds and received his discharge.

Before the war, Baker and Frankie had been living in Georgetown, where Baker had two retail stores. He had sold the stores when he entered the service, but I think he and Frankie had planned to return to Georgetown. However, after things turned out as they did, they decided to settle here in Kingstree, where Baker opened a new furniture business. I had not expected them to change their plans, but it was gratifying to have them living near us.

When peace had finally come after the prolonged tensions of World War II, it took every family a little while to unwind and become readjusted to a life without fear and dread. With us it took longer.

On the day we learned that both Jack and Fred had been killed, we were already sick with worry about Baker's wounds. Our minds instinctively rejected the new blows, recoiling in stunned disbelief. It was impossible for me to grasp the truth, which was contrary to any pattern of civilized life we had known. How could Jack and Fred be dead when we didn't even know where they were? There was nobody to ask anything—nobody to tell us whether they had died instantly, or had lingered and suffered, or had been blown to bits. The Red Cross and politicians in high places could only offer sympathy and promises.

We didn't even have the relief of action to bring full realization to us for there were no arrangements to be made. There were no corpses, no caskets to be selected, no graves to be dug, no funerals to be planned, no pallbearers

Although it recently closed, B.W. Baker Furniture Company served Kingstree for many years from its location on the banks of Black River. *Photograph by Linda Brown.*

to be chosen, no flowers, no doctors to say that everything possible had been done for the boys, no pastors to pronounce benedictions. Nothing. We seemed to be confronted by an enormous void as big as the world, with nothing anywhere for us.

We shed very few tears, and those were only tears of nervous tension. Normal grief couldn't reach through our shock and horror. Nor did we talk as much as usual, but all drew nearer as if each was trying to shield the others in the frightening emptiness around us. Our relatives, pastors and friends were exceedingly kind, but little they said seemed to register with us. Of course, we prayed as usual, or thought we did, but our prayers were just a jumble of words. I suppose that our state of physical shock and fatigue had blocked our mental processes. Each day we went about our usual activities, going to work through force of habit. We had nothing else to do.

Maybe our protective shield of numbness began to crumble when letters we had written to the boys were returned to us stamped with red ink: "Undelivered. Deceased." A few letters that the boys themselves had written weeks earlier were delivered to us. The most recent was from Jack. It was dated March 23, 1945, the day before the Seventeenth Airborne Division made history by parachuting into Germany. Many American boys were shot in mid-air in that engagement, but one of Jack's buddies wrote us months later that he had been with Jack and seen him land safely a little while before he was killed.

Jack was twenty-five the day he wrote the letter. His outfit was then at rest in a camp in France, and the cook had baked him a birthday cake. He got letters from Gladys and his father, but none from Frankie or me. He had spent some idle time stretched out on his blankets listening to a radio broadcast from the United States, the first in a long time. He wrote, in part, "They played 'San Fernando Valley,' 'Rum and Coca Cola,' 'Don't Fence Me In,' 'I'll Be Seeing You,' and other songs I used to be so crazy about. When they played 'God Bless America,' I closed my eyes, thought about home and had a wonderful time."

Though we at home didn't know where Jack and Fred were, the full realization that they were dead finally came through to us. Grief also came into its own. It was devastating beyond anything we could have imagined, but with grief came natural tears, which eased the awesome tensions. Our minds could again reason normally, and we knew we had to take up life as it was, not as it used to be, as there was no choice but to go on from there, to be thankful for the blessings we still had, including the many happy memories of past years which nothing could change.

Only then did we remember the power of prayer to give mortals strength sufficient to bear burdens too heavy to be borne alone. As our mothers and pastors and Sunday-school teachers had taught us through the years, the strength was free for the asking. Nobody had to be a saint to get it and nobody had to make wild promises that couldn't be kept later. Too, I remembered that my mother used to tell her three little daughters never to make the mistake of thinking ourselves privileged characters from whose shoulders all burdens should be lifted—that it was a part of life's plan for everybody to carry a share, that we must learn to carry ours, and it would help us to develop strength and stamina. Only when our burdens became too heavy to be borne alone should we pray for the extra strength, and we would get it. We have found it so.

Mother had also cautioned us to cling always to whatever faith we might have and not to be as unreasonable as the legendary old woman who lived at the foot of the mountain, which she hated because it cut off her view. One night the old woman prayed that the Lord would move the despised mountain. At daybreak the next morning she cracked the door just enough to peep out with one eye. There stood the mountain as usual. She slammed the door angrily and said, "Just as I expected!"

A preacher might say, "Oh, ye of little faith," but I say I hope the poor old soul got a cup of hot coffee or tea. Either can be a very present comfort in moments of disappointment, loneliness or heartbreak.

Material from columns originally published in April 1970.

Mama and the Bootlegger

My youthful father, J.M. Swann, died of appendicitis at our farm home a few months before I was six years old. Mary was eight years old and Eula wasn't quite two.

After Papa died, Mama rented the farm, and she, with her three little girls, moved to Kingstree. Many years later, when this country was in the agonies of Prohibition, she innocently rented the farm to a glib bootlegger, who set up a corn liquor still in Black River swamp on the edge of the farm and was soon doing a thriving business selling White Lightning in half-gallon mason jars at two dollars each.

The frame house that had been our home was headquarters, and a big sign in the front yard said BEWARE OF DOGS, which served two purposes. It was a tip-off to those in the know that liquor was sold there. It was also to make federal agents pause long enough for the bootlegger to hide or destroy the evidence before the premises were searched.

Mary and Eula had married and moved away, but John had bought a two-story frame house on the corner of Live Oak Avenue and Kelley Street in Kingstree, and we, with our small children, were living there. It was a few blocks north of Mama's house on the corner of Academy and Mill Streets.

John and I could have told Mama that her renter was a bootlegger, but as she was handling her own business affairs, she had signed the rent contract before we knew it. We kept quiet to spare her feelings. However, we had to laugh privately because my gentle Mama was a loyal member of the Women's Christian Temperance League.

Mama was dismayed when she finally learned not only that liquor was made in the woods on her land, but also that something had exploded inside the farmhouse and burned it to the ground. The morning after the fire when I went with dread to break the news, she was already hearing it

from Wallace "Skinny" McIntosh, who had stopped by to commiserate with her on the loss of her old home. Wallace, who was about John's age, was a lifelong friend of ours, and he was very fond of Mama.

After greeting me gallantly, he resumed his seat in an easy chair and told Mama that the bootlegger was really a prince of a fellow who sold only pure stuff. Poor Mama managed a faint smile when our eyes met, for she knew that Wallace meant to be kind.

He then glanced around at Mama's home, which was huge and inconvenient and seemed to spread in every direction. "Mrs. Swann, this old house is made of heart lumber and would really make a big fire." She said that was her daily fear, though she had been told that the only way to heat it properly would be to set it afire.

In time it did catch twice, but it was never destroyed, and Mama, who had reached the age to dislike change, continued to keep house there. She died in 1959, but had she lived until August 1960, she would have reached the age of ninety, as had several of her ancestors.

On one of those occasions, it was nothing short of a miracle that it didn't burn down. Mama's cook at the time had a habit of interrupting if Mama happened to have guests. Mama tried time and again to impress upon her not to interrupt conversations in the dining room or elsewhere with remarks of her own.

One day, Mama and a visitor were sitting on the front porch, catching up on the current news when the cook leisurely ambled around the house and stopped near the porch. The visitor, who was the talkative type, kept on and on for some minutes without a break while the cook stood waiting with polite patience.

When the visitor paused to catch a fresh breath, the cook respectfully said, "Mrs. Swann, de top o' you' kitchen is ketched." Fortunately for Mother, it happened in daylight, and the fire was put out before a great deal of damage was done.

I don't remember what became of the bootlegger. Soon after the fire, John and I acquired the farm, and we built a brick home in a beautiful grove of oaks, pines, hollies and dogwoods. We lived there ten years, but during the upheaval of World War II, we decided to move back to our house on Live Oak Avenue and Kelley Street. It still saddens me to ride by the farm. I love every inch of it with its thousand memories, but I've never been sorry we sold it.

Time marches on and conditions change, but tender memories linger to give comfort in these private moments of despair, which come sooner or later to all who live to reach mature years.

Material from columns originally published in February 1971.

Moving

One balmy night when John and I were nearing fifty years old, we had put on bathrobes and were sitting in our usual rocking chairs on an upstairs porch that opened off our bedroom at the corner of Live Oak Avenue and Kelley Street in Kingstree. When he remarked idly that our house was too big for only two people and I agreed, he went on to say that old age was around the corner, and that sooner or later one of us would drop off, leaving the other to rattle around alone in that big place.

"You wouldn't rattle long," I teased, as he hated to be alone even a half-hour. "But please don't copy Mr. So-and-So." He chuckled at the memory of a man we once knew who had tried to jump into his first wife's grave, but within three weeks was courting another. "And promise me," I said, "not to marry an eighteen-year-old."

John held up his right hand. "I promise. I like them sixteen."

"All right, Mr. Smarty," I retorted, "but some night you will be rocking alone by my empty chair and wondering which handsome young buck is skylarking with your child bride who is supposed to be sitting with her ailing grandma. If you hear a strange sound, like a ghost laughing, that will be me."

However, we decided seriously that same night to be on the lookout for a vacant lot or a smaller house for sale, preferably within walking distance of the business district in case we wouldn't always be able to use a car.

It wasn't long before the one-story white cottage, where I now live on the corner of Academy and Church Streets, was sold at auction to settle an estate, and John bought it. Though the house, which is one of the oldest in Kingstree, was in a dilapidated condition, it was structurally sound. Thanks to L.K. Montgomery, architect, and Sam McKenzie, contractor, we got a comfortable and roomy home that both of us lived to enjoy a good many years.

John and Bessie Britton at John's seventy-first birthday dinner in 1962. *Photograph courtesy of Williamsburgh Historical Museum.*

No doubt I was a nuisance hanging around the workmen, most of whom I had known a long time, but I enjoyed watching their progress. I had an active imagination and knew exactly how the finished job would look. Besides, I enjoyed the workmen's happy-go-lucky humor, and if my presence cramped their style, they were too polite to show it.

The cottage on Academy Street is still identified by many townspeople as "Miss Bessie" Britton's house. *Photograph by Linda Brown.*

However, John didn't have much patience, and he couldn't bear to watch slow, tedious work. One morning he came back from his office downtown to see what had been accomplished since his last visit a few days earlier. He watched the workmen's leisurely pace a few minutes in silent torment, then he blew a gasket and cussed out the crowd and stormed out the door without so much as a goodbye to me. I was embarrassed, but not the workmen. They laughed, and none took offense. They knew him well. Besides, they knew that John was a soft touch when any of them needed help to get out of a jam, which seemed remarkably often.

Once I was reconciled to the idea of leaving the old house with its many memories, I could hardly wait to move in and get settled before Christmas (which we did). I was uneasy and wanted every day to count. So one morning I nearly blew a gasket when not a soul showed up at the job except the architect and me. All had decided to take the day off to go duck shooting. Also, I got a bad fright the time one of Mr. McKenzie's small sons hid inside the cement mixer but was rescued in the nick of time.

One of the painters was a tall, lanky old bachelor from Lane with a dry wit. He liked his gin, but he didn't like the subdued colors I had chosen for the living room and dining room, or he pretended he didn't. He kept asking me to let him use brighter colors, or at least not to paint both rooms alike even though they adjoined and had wide, double doors between them. Another day when he was on a ladder painting a high ceiling, he paused with brush in hand and looked down to ask how much I weighed.

"A hundred and twenty pounds," I replied.

He shook his head dolefully. "Next year you will weigh a hundred and one pounds." When I didn't answer, he asked, "Have you ever counted the windows in this joint?"

"Yes, indeed," I rose to the bait. "All nineteen of them, but each seems to serve a purpose."

He turned back to his work, mumbling to himself in singsong tones, "Nineteen purposes. Nineteen purposes. To be washed. In the spring and fall."

Going back still further, when we first lived in the old house from which we moved to the cottage, our two children were small and all the bedrooms were upstairs. One night when Frankie was nine and Jack was five years old, I went upstairs to put Jack to bed in his own room, which was all right with him as he wasn't a scary child. John and Frankie were reading in the living room downstairs.

As usual, I told Jack a bedtime story and I listened to his long prayers, in which he blessed every relative and most of his friends by name, including the neighborhood dogs and cats. By the time he had finished, he was sleepy (and I was exhausted). After a few more delaying goodnight kisses, he didn't mind being left alone with a light burning in the hall.

I had just settled down with John and Frankie when Jack, who had a comically deep voice for such a little fellow, let out a bellow that could be heard all over the place. "Mother," he bawled, "come back here and get God out of my room. I'd rather be by myself."

At that, the rest of us went upstairs for the night.

Material from columns originally published in February 1971.

The Christmas Eve Explosion

In mid-December 1961, John and I were living in the white cottage where I now live on the corner of Academy and Church Streets in Kingstree. One rainy night after we had finished the last of the Christmas decorations in the living room and dining room, John said he was going to take a shower and put on his formal evening clothes. That meant his pajamas and a shabby, old maroon lounging robe, which he had refused to discard because it was so comfortable.

When he came back, I was rearranging a centerpiece in the dining room. He took his seat at one end of the oblong table and began playing solitaire. After threatening to kill him if he disturbed the centerpiece, I kicked off my high heels and flopped into an easy chair with a magazine that described the childhood Christmases best remembered by several men and women of national prominence. There wasn't a sound to be heard except the slap-slap of John's cards on the polished table. The game was relaxing to him, and he could play for hours, or maybe it was just that I couldn't keep quiet that long. "John," I asked, "which Christmas gave you the biggest bang when you were a child?"

He laughed and said without hesitation, "It was the Christmas a group of little boys made the Confederate cannon bang on the courthouse square, and I got a licking for my part in it." He put the cards down, lit a cigarette and asked if I wanted to hear about it. I said yes, but to wait until I had put on my evening clothes, too.

A Confederate cannon, which is now mounted on a permanent base at the Williamsburg County Courthouse, was then mounted on its original caisson, which had huge wooden wheels with iron rims, and could be shifted to different positions on the courthouse square.

The small sons of elected officials who had offices inside the courthouse liked to play on the cannon. I don't remember whose bright idea it was to make secret plans to fire it at dusk on Christmas Eve.

The old cannon is still mounted in the Courthouse Square. *Photograph by Linda Brown.*

County auditor J.J.B. Montgomery's sons were Benton, Sam John, Donald and Zeno, but I think John said only Sam John and Donald were among the culprits. Superintendent of Education J.G. McCullough had several sons, and Dr. Jack McCullough might have been in on the mischief and also Treasurer J.W. Cook's oldest son, Earle. Probate Judge S.M Scott's sons were too old, but Magistrate John Gamble's son, Frank, might have been among the guilty; likewise, Sheriff G.J. Graham's little son, Willie. But Supervisor J.N. Hammet's only son George was then too young to be trusted not to tell the big secret.

Clerk of Court H.O. Britton's sons were Harry, John and Billie. I doubt that Harry, who was a steady, quiet fellow, joined in the mischief, but he would not have told on the younger boys. In fact, he talked so little, he would hardly tell you the time of day. No doubt Billie Britton, youngest of the brothers, was among the culprits, though he might not care to admit it now.

Of course, the little boys had never heard a cannon go off, and they knew nothing about loading one, much less firing one, but they knew it was gunpowder that made such thrilling noise when stumps were blasted. They managed somehow to get an unknown quantity of it to mix with brickbats and old iron nails, and they packed the cannon full. I don't know who lit

The Williamsburg County Courthouse as it looks today. *Photograph by Linda Brown.*

Mr. Donald Montgomery (*right*) who succeeded his father as county auditor, with Sam John's son Zeno. *Photograph courtesy of Linda Brown.*

the match, but the good Lord was with him. Otherwise, he and his buddies hovering close by would have been blown to kingdom come.

The cannon went off with such a roar that people as far distant as Salters thought the Yankees had launched a new attack. A few nervous Nellies took to the woods, but able-bodied men from every direction grabbed their guns, jumped on their horses and galloped to Kingstree, ready to fight again.

By a miracle, the explosion did no serious damage, so a great time was had by all except the small culprits. The roar of the cannon had scared them half-witted, and insult was added to injury when they got their little bottoms nearly blistered as a Christmas bonus.

Material from columns originally published in March 1971.

A Visit from Mrs. Santa Claus

The next night, John was reading in an easy chair before the fireplace in the living room and I was seated nearby, checking a list of things yet to be done before Christmas.

He put *Detective Magazine* down to light a cigarette and asked which had been the most exciting Christmas I could remember. I thought a moment. "It was when I was five years old, the year before Papa died."

He asked what had happened, and that was all I needed to regale him with the story.

My family was then living on the farm three miles from Kingstree. Those were days of leisurely living. There were no telephones, no electricity, no cars, no paved roads and no RFD (Rural Free Delivery) mail. A farmer usually sent a plowboy on horseback to the post office in Kingstree for the mail.

People who wanted to travel farther than a horse or canoe could carry them had to make the trip in the dirty coaches of slow trains on the Atlantic Coast Line Railroad, now the Seaboard Coastline Railroad. There was a small, wooden station called the depot about a mile north of the present brick station. When friends or relatives came from a distance, they stayed at least a month and were welcome.

Our guests that Christmas were two exceptionally pretty girls about nineteen, a true brunette and a true blonde, who were devoted to each other. Curls were very much in style, and both girls had been blessed with an abundance of naturally curly hair. The brunette was Katherine Lewis, who was my mother's sister. The blonde was Caroline Cox, who was my father's niece. Mrs. Gaynelle Gamble Hammet is her daughter. Gay was named by her mother after the heroine in a Victorian novel, but Gay was only seven months old when Caroline died.

Mama and the visitors had a bright idea for Christmas—at least they thought it bright at the time. My sister, Mary, was nearly eight, but Eula was only a year old. Mary and I were told that Mrs. Santa Claus was coming to call about dusk Christmas Eve, and we could invite her to stay over for our tree.

We had the stockings Christmas morning. The tree in the corner of the large sitting room had been decorated with strings of popcorn grown on the farm, colored paper chains made at home and also wild seed pods gathered from ditch banks in the fall and dyed bright colors at home. The small candles of beeswax molded at home had bits of bayberry leaves in them for fragrance. And there were many tiny lambs made at home of fluffy white cotton. I wanted a little lamb very much but never got one, possibly because the same lambs were used year after year.

Mr. Santa Claus himself would be too busy guiding his reindeer hither and yon to stop with his wife, but he would return before daylight with three doll babies for our stockings, which would be hung by the chimney with care. In the meantime, Mary and I must be on our good behavior, and Mrs. Santa Claus would stay for refreshments before rejoining her husband. The refreshments were calf's-foot jelly tinted with red beet juice and topped with whipped cream in our best saucers. A pound cake, which had been baked with a fresh, green leaf clipped from a potted rose geranium in the bottom of the pan for aroma, had thick, white icing. Also, there was hot sassafras tea with dried lemon peel and brown sugar, which was made from cane grown on the farm. Sassafras was an aromatic shrub growing wild in low places. Tea brewed from its roots had a delightful bouquet and was good for what ailed you, whether a broken heart or an upset stomach.

John interrupted my harangue to ask how in heck did Mary and I think that Mrs. Santa Claus would get to our house. Or would her ever-loving husband just pitch her off the sleigh as he flew over and let nature take its course? Mary and I were too excited to wonder. We could think only of good old Santa Claus striving to please, and reindeer flying with the greatest of ease. But we believed that the right name was Sandy Claws. We had spent hours every day of our lives with the Gullah-speaking Negroes on the farm, and that's what they called St. Nick, so we did, too.

Before Mrs. Santa Claus arrived, Mary, Eula and I were well scrubbed in the big wooden tub before an open fire that threatened to blister us on one side while the other side nearly froze. Our long, cotton flannel nightgowns with high necks and long sleeves were warming by the fire. To keep our faces and hands from chapping after the baths, they were daintily rubbed with a small cake of beef tallow that had been molded at home in a fluted muffin tin. Crushed rose petals had been added to it to compete with the cow smell.

Finally, Mary and I were settled in our small rocking chairs, made of white oak strips by a basketweaver on the farm, and told to stay put. Eula was cuddled in Mama's lap. Papa, who was in his usual big chair watching with amusement the activities of his house full of females, must have wished for at least one other male—if only Mr. Sandy Claws.

There was no such thing as a bought false face, but there was such a thing as a doughface—which was seldom put to use, as it was so messy—and we had never seen one. A doughface was a mask made by fitting a thin layer of raw biscuit dough over a victim's face, with slits for the eyes, nostrils and mouth.

Mary and I didn't notice that blonde Caroline and brunette Katherine were nowhere to be seen. The girls were in the kitchen giggling. Presently Caroline appeared in the doorway, her cheeks flushed pink. She looked like a doll in her long blue dress with a wide belt cinched around her trim waist. She announced to Papa that Mrs. Santa Claus had arrived and was in the kitchen, of all places. Maybe Caroline expected my handsome Papa to rise gallantly and escort the lady in, but he only laughed and kept his place as a spectator and not a participant in that circus, which had been the women's idea in the first place.

My pretty Aunt Katherine had always called me Bess, and I called her Katty. When she came tripping in from the kitchen, her long red dress was set off by a perky black hat with a lace veil hanging off the back. She wore black kid gloves and high-button shoes—and a dead, white doughface. I didn't recognize Katty, but I knew a ghost when I saw one drained of blood and looking for a sinner. I gave a shriek of raw terror and bolted through the opposite door, screaming with every breath. I tumbled down the steps, picked myself up and sped down the avenue toward the public road. I didn't know where I was going, but I was on my way. Katty forgot the doughface and took out after me, calling, "Bess, wait for me." That put wings on my feet.

Indoors, pandemonium had broken loose. Mama was vainly trying to pacify Eula, who was wailing like a banshee. Poor little Mary, who was always a sedate child, had dashed to the far corner of the room and pressed her face into the angle, sobbing with her every breath. She, too, knew a ghost when she saw one looking for a sinner. Caroline ran to comfort her, but Caroline's hand on Mary's shoulder had set her to shrieking, too.

Katty, who was fleet of foot, finally overtook me and held me kicking and screaming until I was exhausted before I recognized her voice. She carried me back in her arms, gently crooning for me to be a sweet baby and hush my crying, and I could have two little cups of sassafras tea. By that time, Caroline had calmed Mary, and Mama had calmed the baby.

What was my big, strong Papa doing all this time to help his family in distress? Not one blessed thing. He was absolutely helpless with laughter. But the women weren't even smiling. When Katty began peeling that dough from her face, it came off in strings, which she tossed into the fire. They smelled like biscuits scorching.

While Mama and Caroline helped Katty, Papa, with Eula in his lap, watched silently, but no doubt he had to wipe his eyes now and then. By that time, Mary and I were also laughing at the show, but the women still saw nothing to smile about.

Papa got himself another cup of hot tea. Eula immediately kicked the cup over, and the tea spilled into his lap. He wouldn't let on that he minded, possibly because the women had then begun laughing hysterically.

As I finished the story by telling John that Santa Claus brought three dolls, he said, "That Christmas takes the rag off the bush. Why didn't you tell me about it before now?"

"I don't know," I said. "Unless for the same reason that you never told me about the cannon until last night. But do you know something, Honey," I added seriously, "our generation will never run out of I-remember-whens. There was a lot of creative action when people had to make do with what they had. Families hated debt worse than a plague, and the average man's word was as good as his bond. I wonder if children in those days didn't have as much fun making up their own games as children now have in organized activities. A few new toys once a year must have been more thrilling than several new toys every week. And those storybooks were beloved possessions to be treasured for life. Oh, well. It was nice while it lasted."

John looked pensive. "I'll say amen to that sermon."

I glanced at my watch and got up. "It's time for our bedtime snack. Modern food in a modern kitchen, but I thank the Lord it's modern—I guess."

As John got up, too, he asked, "What did that elegant calf's-foot jelly taste like?"

I said, "Jello."

He burst out laughing and said, well, he'd be a so-and-so, but his exact words don't bear repeating in a family newspaper. John had a remarkable flow of language under stress of emotion, but much of it wouldn't do to print.

Material from columns originally published in March 1971.